Reading & Critical Thinking Book 2

by Donald L. Barnes, Ed.D.
Arlene Burgdorf, Ed.D.
and Laura L. Helms

Educational Design,Inc., 47 West 13 Street, New York, NY 10011.
ISBN # 0-87694-000-9 EDI 332

EDUCATIONAL DESIGN, INC. EDI 332

Table of Contents

A. Literal Thinking Skills
B. Inferential Thinking Skills
C. Evaluative Thinking Skills

This book is about two things—reading and thinking. These two things are really one. Thinking makes it possible for you to understand what you read. The better your thinking skills, the better you can read. This book will help you sharpen your reading and thinking skills.

The first ten chapters in this book concentrate on three groups of skills. They are Literal Reading Skills, Inferential Thinking Skills, and Evaluative Thinking Skills.

Literal Reading Skills are the ones you use to understand the basic meaning of what you read. The beginning chapter gives you practice on one of the most important: cause-effect relationships.

Inferential Thinking Skills go a step further. "Inferential" means "inferring"—that is, making a good guess. When you infer something, it means that you have reasoned that something is true without actually being told. Five chapters concentrate on these thinking skills, which are vital to a full understanding of what you read.

Evaluative Thinking Skills are the ones you use when you form opinions and make decisions. You use these skills when you compare one idea with another. Telling the difference between a fact and an opinion in a piece of writing is an evaluative skill. So is spotting the author's point of view.

Each of the first ten chapters in this book is organized the same way. The chapter begins with an explanation of what the skill is and contains some practice exercises for you to work with. Then come stories with questions to give you understanding and practice on the skill. When you have completed these chapters, you will be able to handle the more difficult stories that follow.

1. Cause-Effect Relationships

People are constantly looking for causes. When someone is injured, we want to know how or why the accident happened. When large numbers of people in a town get sick, we want to know if the air, the water, the food, or some type of pollution has caused the illness.

It is easy to make mistakes in looking for causes. There can be at least four problems:

A. Just because two events happen one after another does ***not*** mean that the first causes the second to happen. A train may whistle just before it enters a town, but the whistle doesn't cause the train to go through the town. A dog may walk around in small circles before it lies down. Walking in circles, however, doesn't cause the dog to lie down.

B. Secondly, there are things which are ***necessary preconditions***, but not direct causes. We may say that we will play baseball on Tuesday if it isn't raining. However, clear weather doesn't cause us to play baseball; it just makes it possible for us to play. Likewise, we may say that we can't buy a candy bar unless we have money. Having money, however, doesn't cause us to buy a candy bar.

C. Thirdly, we should recognize that some causes are ***direct*** and others are ***indirect***. If Jerry hits Jack in the face, causing Jack's lip to bleed, Jack may go to the nurse's office. In this situation, we cannot say that Jerry caused Jack to go to the nurse, but we can say that Jerry caused Jack's lip to bleed. Likewise, in another situation, Tom stayed up late watching TV and did poorly on the history test the next day. Staying up late doesn't always cause people to do poorly on history tests. We can reasonably assume, however, that Tom's TV watching indirectly affected his school work.

D. Finally, we must recognize that most events have ***multiple causes***. When you turn on the light switch in your bedroom, you may think that you are causing the light to go on. There are, however, lots of things that must also take place in order for the light to go on. The generating plants must be working; the transmission wires must be operating correctly; the fuses in your fuse box must be in place.

1. See if you can pick out the five cause-effect statements in the sentences below.

a. The wind blew and the rain came down in torrents as the baby was born.
b. As the birds flew in through the open door, the clock began to chime.
c. Many of the waterfowl were ill because chemicals had been sprayed on their nesting areas.
d. Her "hay fever" is the result of the face powder she uses.
e. As the factory whistle blew, the club members were gathering for a meeting.
f. The corn had been picked late, and it was almost too hard to eat.
g. The gully deepened as the torrents of rain continued to come down.
h. A bolt of lightning struck the tree and split it wide open.

Answers: Did you put checks beside c,d,f,g, and h? These are the correct answers.

You will recall that necessary preconditions don't actually make things happen, but they are required before an event can take place.

2. Select the five statements below which describe *necessary preconditions*, but not actual causes.

a. To continue to live, you must breathe air.
b. You must go to where the artist is singing if you wish to hear his songs.
c. The riots were caused by the people who had no jobs.
d. If you get more workers, the project will move along quickly.
e. To become President of the United States, a candidate must first be nominated at the party's nominating convention.
f. Mary needed to get permission before she could leave school.
g. Time will cure all ills.
h. Weeds were growing all over and choking the plants.

Answers: Did you put checks beside a, b, d, e and f?

You will remember that *direct* causes bring about specific, highly-predictable effects (results). *Indirect* causes set a series of events in motion, but some of the effects may not be highly predicable.

3. Select the five statements below which describe *indirect* causes.

a. Tom Jackson lost Bill's football letter, and Bill avoided him for the rest of the school year.
b. Arlene liked the picture. She went out and bought copies for all of her friends.
c. Jane hid Tom's books.
d. Tim Wilson made an error that lost the game for his side. When he got home he didn't feel like eating.
e. Al Roberts lost the book he was supposed to study for the final exam. He got a lousy grade in the course.
f. Jose liked baseball better that any other sport.
g. Sally dropped her fork, leaned over to pick it up, and fell onto the floor.
h. Robert broke the school swimming record.

Answers: Did you put checks beside a, b, d, e, and g?

You will remember that many events have multiple causes. In other words, several factors bring about the results.

4. Select the five statements below which describe *multiple causes*.

a. The hot sun and the searing wind dried up the plants.
b. The tire on the bike was punctured by a nail.
c. The lamp fell to the floor and broke.
d. The driver couldn't see in the heavy rainstorm, the brakes suddenly failed, and the truck rammed into a tree.

e. The drop in temperature resulted in the use of more oil and higher heating bills.
f. The picture could hardly be seen because the colors were dark and the light was dim.
g. Dennis was confused and very frightened and couldn't develop a plan of escape.
h. With his new promotion, better working conditions, and higher pay, Charles felt very happy.

Answers: Did you put checks beside a, d, f, g, and h?

It is also important to realize that not all results are of equal importance. If large numbers of people are influenced and if the results relate to very important human goals, we may consider them crucial. The development of vaccines to fight diseases, for example, has influenced the lives of millions of people.

RACING OVER THE ICE

When Roald Amundsen (AH mund sun) of Norway was a boy, he dreamed of being the first person to reach the North Pole. As a young man he tried to condition himself for the hardships he knew he would face on such a trip. He lifted weights to build up his muscles. He slept in the cold Norwegian winters with windows of his bedroom wide open. When he entered adulthood, he continued to prepare for his dreamed-of trip. He now began to seek financial support for his venture. Finally when he was 32, he had the ships, supplies, and strength for his journey. But Amundsen was too late! United States Navy Commodore Robert E. Peary had already reached the North Pole.

Amundsen was discouraged, but he didn't give up. He quickly changed his plans. He joined in a deadly race with British Commander Robert F. Scott to be the first to reach the South Pole. Commander Scott had come within 555 miles of the South Pole just eight years before but had to turn back.

On October 20, 1911, Amundsen set out with four companions, four sleds, 52 huskies, and supplies to last four months. The party traveled up to 29 miles a day, an amazing achievement over such difficult terrain in the bitter harsh cold of the Antarctic. Almost two months later, on December 14, Amundsen and his companions reached their goal.

Scott and his party did not know of Amundsen's success. They were actually more than a month behind Amundsen's pace. Faced with fierce storms, severe cold, semi-darkness, and dangerous terrain, Scott and his men finally reached their goal on January 18, 1912. Much to their sorrow they found Amundsen's Norwegian flag already there. Depressed, hungry, and weak, Scott and his party started the long trip home. They never reached their destination. All five members of the expedition died on the return trip.

QUESTIONS

1. Identify two of what Amundsen thought were *necessary preconditions* for a successful trip to the North Pole.

____

____

2. How did Commodore Peary's explorations *indirectly cause* Amundsen to change his destination?

____

____

____

3. There were *multiple causes* of the hardships which both Amundsen and Scott endured on their trips to the South Pole. What were these multiple causes?

____

____

____

MICROWAVE MANIA

A microwave in electronics is a very short electromagnetic wave, that is, a wave with a super-high frequency. The wavelength of microwaves is indeed much shorter than that used in commercial radio broadcasting.

One of the important uses of microwaves is radar (radio detection and ranging). Radar was used in World War II to track airplanes. It has since been used for storm tracking, air-traffic control, surveying, and satellite and rocket guidance. Microwaves are also used to carry information for telephone and television systems.

One advantage of microwaves is that they can carry more information than radio waves. A disadvantage is that they are not reflected back from the upper atmosphere, so they cannot reach beyond the horizon.

The use of microwaves that you may be most familiar with is the microwave oven, an electronic oven which cooks food by means of the heat produced from microwave penetration. This appliance has continued to grow in popularity at a very rapid rate. Approximately eight and one-half million microwave ovens are sold annually in the United States alone. More than 50 percent of all American homes are thought to be equipped with microwave ovens. This is double the number that were microwave-equipped in 1982.

When microwave ovens were introduced, many people thought they were unsafe. Concerns about safety hazards have diminished. Since 1971 these appliances have had to meet safety standards set by the Food and Drug Administration. Among other things, the FDA requires all ovens to have two independent interlocking doors. They will not operate unless both doors are closed.

Microwave ovens are no longer a luxury. In fact, they are considered by many people a necessity like washers or refrigerators. One reason is that Americans are spending less time in the kitchen, and microwave ovens cook food in 1/2 to 1/8 the time of regular ovens. They heat prepared frozen meals in a few minutes. They re-heat food and liquids rapidly. To heat a cup of liquid takes one minute. An early problem of unevenly cooked food has been virtually eliminated. Food cooked by microwave is tasty and has been found to be as safe to eat as food cooked in a regular oven.

"Microwave mania" has taken over as one of the strongest consumer trends.

QUESTIONS

Each of the statements below involves something other than a direct cause-effect relationship. In the blank following each statement, write the name of the relationship. Your choices are: ***NO VALID CAUSE***, ***NECESSARY PRECONDITION***, ***INDIRECT CAUSE***, ***ONLY ONE OF MANY CAUSES.***

1. Your brother became sick after standing in front of your microwave.

   ____

2. Americans generally are spending less time in the kitchen; microwave ovens have grown in popularity.

   ____

3. Microwave sales have increased, and frozen food sales have doubled.

____

4. Radar is used to track a storm; then the storm destroys a town.

____

5. Microwaves are no longer a luxury. The FDA requires microwaves to meet safety standards.

____

6. The FDA requires all microwave ovens to meet safety standards; concerns about safety hazards have diminished.

____

A LIGHTNING CURE

Long-distance truck driver Edwin Robinson had a bad accident on the road when he was 53 years old. The accident left him blind and almost deaf. He had no hope of recovery.

All of this changed on a rainy day in June of 1980. Robinson decided to check on his pet chicken Took-Took, which was outside in the yard. He carried an aluminum cane because of his blindness, and he was wearing his hearing aid. As he passed under a poplar tree, a bolt of lightning knocked him unconscious. He awoke 20 minutes later to discover that he could again see, even better than before the accident, and that his hearing was fully restored!

His ophthalmologist didn't know how to explain all of this at first. Then he said, "It's a miracle. I don't know why it happened, but I think the change is permanent. Shocks do strange things."

Robinson remarked after the event, "I'm all recharged now, literally." A month after the incident, hair began to sprout on his bald head! "It's coming in thick," he related. "My wife doesn't know what to make of it. I was bald for 35 years."

There were two casualties from the bolt of lightning: Robinson's hearing device was completely burned out, and so was the poplar tree.

QUESTIONS

1. Which of the following statements contain cause-effect relationships?

a. Edwin Robinson was 53, and he had a bad truck accident.
b. After the accident, Robinson became blind and almost deaf.
c. When he walked under the poplar tree, a bolt of lightning knocked him unconscious.
d. He carried an aluminum cane because of his blindness.
e. Took-Took was outside in the yard when the lightning hit.
f. After he was hit by lightning, Robinson could see and hear again.

In addition to there being *multiple causes* of a single effect, there are also *multiple effects* from a single cause. For example, catching a cold may cause you to sneeze, to run a fever, and to develop chills.

2. Which statements below show *multiple effects* coming from a single cause?

a. There were two casualties from the bolt of lightning: Robinson's hearing device was completely burned out, and so was the poplar tree.
b. Lightning knocked Robinson unconscious and restored his hearing.
c. A bad accident on the road left him blind and deaf.
d. The shock caused his hair to grow again.

STOPPED BY A METEORITE

In the year 1907 a military group was seeking to win its way into power in Nicaragua. The rebels were led by General Pablo Castilliano. He had weapons, money, and a background of excellent military training.

General Castilliano and his forces had twice defeated government troops and were planning a final assault the next morning. The general retired to his tent to record the day's events. At about ten in the evening he blew out his candle and went to bed.

Only minutes later the sky was lit by a flaming mass streaking down out of a clear sky—and heading straight for the camp. The terrified guard outside the general's tent threw himself to the ground.

The ball of fire flew straight into General Castilliano's tent with a terrific roar. It blasted out a pit 10 feet deep and about 15 feet in diameter. The general died instantly. His guard lived for two hours and was able to state that the hole was a result of a fireball from the sky. Pieces of shattered meteorite were found in the pit.

The general's death sent the troops into complete disarray. They took it as a sign of heaven's disfavor, and the revolt collapsed. This is the only war known to have been brought to an end by an object from the heavens.

QUESTIONS

1. The sentences at the left are causes of events in the story. At the right are the effects of those causes. Match the proper effect to each cause.

______The sky was lit with the fire from the meteorite.	a. The troops became disorganized.
______The meteorite struck the general's tent.	b. The general died.
______The soldiers believed the meteorite was a sign from heaven.	c. The general's guard became terrified and fell to the ground.

2. "This is the only war known to have been brought to an end by an object from the heavens." This statement is an example of —

a. Necessary precondition
b. Indirect cause
c. Multiple causes

3. Which of the following statements shows *indirect* cause-effect relationship? (Check one or more.)

a. The guard lived two hours and was able to tell what happened.
b. The general retired to his tent early, which allowed him to write down the day's events.
c. The terrified guard saw the meteorite outside of the general's tent and threw himself to the ground.

4. Which of the following are *necessary preconditions* to a successful military campaign?

a. Weapons need to be available.
b. Money must be provided.
c. The leader needs to know how to direct military operations.
d. A candle needs to be provided in the leader's tent.
e. A guard must be posted outside of the leader's tent.
f. There needs to be a tent for the leader.
g. There must be soldiers to fight battles.

2. Detecting Assumptions and Evaluating Conclusions

An author's discussion is often based upon hidden assumptions. To understand fully what you are reading, your first job may well be to detect any such hidden assumptions. Then you can check for the reasonableness, not only of the assumptions, but also of any conclusions it helps to support.

Look over this example:

> When the three of us graduate in June we should have a party.

The assumption in this example is that the three of you will graduate. The key word here is "when."

Here is another example:

> You can get by this afternoon dressed in shirtsleeves, but I would take along a sweater this evening.

The assumption here is that it will get colder in the evening.

Now see if you can find the hidden assumption in each of the following statements.

1. When the world finally gets rid of the atom bomb, it will be a much better place to live in.

What is the hidden assumption in this statement?

a. The atom bomb will always be with us.
b. The atom bomb will destroy the world.
c. The world will get rid of the atom bomb.

2. Since you were able to learn French so easily, I don't know why you say German is such a tough language.

What is the hidden assumption?

a. French is an easy language.
b. German is a tough language.
c. German is not a lot tougher than French.

3. For some reason, Hitler decided not to invade England. This cost him the war.

The author appears to assume that—

a. An invasion of England would have been successful.
b. Hitler was a brilliant strategist.
c. England would have fought to the end.

Answers: 1.c, 2.c, 3.a

Detecting and evaluating assumptions is one task the intelligent reader has. A second task is to evaluate conclusions or explanations.

There are two keys to checking such conclusions or explanations:

I. The person doing the evaluating must, first of all, have some knowledge of the subject or situation. Knowledgeable individuals can make better judgments than uninformed people. It is almost impossible to know whether a conclusion is accurate if you are poorly informed.

II. Secondly, there needs to be some check on the reasonableness or logic of the explanation. Does the reasoning behind the conclusion make sense? Does it appear that the person making the conclusion or explanation really considered all of the many aspects of the problem? For example, if we can't get a desk lamp to work, we may test the light bulb to see if it is burned out. If the light bulb works properly, we may check the wall plug to see if the electricity has been disrupted or turned off. Only after checking these various possibilities is it safe to conclude that the lamp is broken.

The most common mistake people make in evaluating a set of conclusions is that they don't take into consideration the wide range of possible explanations for what has been observed. In other words, they are too quickly satisfied with easy answers. A small boy may see men putting up a huge tent on the main street of his town. The boy's playmate tells him that there must be a circus in town. The small boy quickly accepts the explanation. He does not realize that the tent could be used for religious services, a wedding reception, a display of new cars, a hobby show, the presentation of a play, or any number of other community activities.

In each of the situations below, you are given one possible explanation for what you are observing. See if you can think of one or two additional explanations.

1. You see an abandoned car beside the road. Your brother says he believes the driver must have run out of gas. What other explanation could there be?

____

____

2. There is a long line of people outside a store. Your mom says that she thinks the store is giving away free samples of something. What other explanation could there be?

____

____

3. You come upon a child crying in the city park. Your brother says that he thinks the child is crying because he is lost. What other explanation could there be?

____

____

4. There is a strange dog hanging around your yard. A neighbor says that she believes a passing motorist has abandoned the dog. What other explanation could there be?

____

____

5. You have observed moving lights in the woods behind your house. A friend who is visiting you says that she thinks people with flashlights are looking for animals in the woods. What other explanation could there be?

____

____

6. You observe an old gentleman in the park throw down a newspaper and jump on it with both feet. A friend who also observed the happening says that she thinks the old man was disgusted with something he read in the paper. What other explanation could there be for his behavior?

____

____

Answer: Some other possible explanations for the events you observed: The car in the first situation could be disabled; the long line of people at the store may be wanting to buy something that is in short supply; the crying child in the city park may be unhappy because he has lost a favorite toy; the strange dog in your yard may simply be hungry; the lights in the woods may be from people who are searching for a lost item; the gentleman who threw down the paper may have just remembered something he was supposed to do, and he is disgusted with himself, not the paper.

THE MYSTERY OF THE BERMUDA TRIANGLE

At two o'clock on the afternoon of December 5, 1945, five United States bombers left Fort Lauderdale, Florida. There were 14 people aboard the planes.

Suddenly, the head of the group contacted the tower at Fort Lauderdale. The officer said that he thought they must be off course. He could not tell where they were. Then he said, "Looks like we are —." He gave no more information. His plane and the other four aircraft were never seen again.

A Martin flying boat with 13 people was sent to find the planes. The flying boat sent one radio message. After that the Martin was never heard from again. Next, Coast Guard ships searched the sea where they thought the planes went down. They found no oil slicks. There were no flares. There was no wreckage.

All night the search continued. In the morning, 255 planes flew over the area. They found no traces of the missing aircraft.

This part of the Atlantic Ocean is called the Bermuda Triangle. Dozens of ships have disappeared there over the centuries. One possible explanation is that unusual weather sometimes covers the area. Storms can develop very quickly.

The mystery has not been solved. Other ships and planes have since been lost in the area from time to time. The U.S. believes that all of these disasters were unusual happenings. But they do not believe that there are "strange forces" at work.

QUESTIONS

1. The selection says that one possible explanation is that unusual weather sometimes covers the area.

The author appears to assume that—

a. Unusual weather could cause the type of occurrences described.
b. It is not certain that unusual weather sometimes covers the area.
c. Unusual weather is itself a "strange force."

2. Very unusual weather patterns near Bermuda have been cited as causes of these accidents. What other explanations might there be?

____

____

____

3. If someone suggested that a monster had destroyed the planes, would you accept the explanation? Why or why not?

____

____

4. If a friend read that UFO's had destroyed the planes, would you accept the explanation? Why or why not?

____

____

HIGH-TECH CERAMICS

Since 1975 chemists have learned to blend, beat, and bake various ceramic compounds into materials that are: stronger than steel; as hard as diamonds; and tough enough to withstand the heat of a blast furnace.

Medicine, aerospace, transportation, and electronics are using ceramics in ways no one could possibly have imagined just a few decades ago. High-tech ceramics have begun to appear in batteries, bearings, fuel cells, gas engines, resistors, solar cells, tape recorders, and a host of other products. Probably the most exciting use is a tiny computer of ceramic that runs on laser light instead of electricity!

The manufacturing of the new ceramics is unlike the old process of molding and firing plain clay. It begins with pure, ultrafine particles of aluminum or titanium oxide, sand, feldspar, and other minerals and chemicals. These are carefully mixed, formed, fired, and treated under closely regulated processes.

One important advance in ceramics has increased the sensitivity of the Navy's sonar and hydrophones (underwater microphones that can pick up the sounds of ships and submarines) about a thousand times!

A futuristic device being studied is the ceramic automobile engine. It would be smaller, lighter, and cheaper and able to run at hotter temperatures than engines made of metal. The high temperatures alone would make fuel 30 percent more efficient.

QUESTIONS

1. Which of the following conclusions is supported by information in the first paragraph?

   a. Ceramic compounds are formed into material by applying heat only.
   b. Diamonds are very hard gems.
   c. The heat from a blast furnace is not very hot.

In each of the following pairs of statements, decide which conclusion is ***NOT*** supported by information in the story.

2. a. One of the biggest uses of high-tech ceramics is in art pottery.
   b. High-tech ceramics are used for certain things that used to use metal.

3. a. Some automobile parts are made with high-tech ceramics.
   b. One of the main advantages of high-tech ceramics is that they are cheap.

4. a. The production of high-tech ceramics is a complicated process.
   b. The new ceramics are more beautiful than the old ceramics.

5. a. High-tech ceramics are useful only in large products.
   b. High-tech ceramics are manufactured from a mixture of several ingredients.

6. Which of the following is a valid conclusion based on the information in the story?

   a. A large percentage of new cars have ceramic engines.
   b. People who like big cars would not like cars with ceramic engines.
   c. One of the potential advantages of a ceramic car engine is that it might be considerably cheaper to operate.

7. The author says that, "The manufacturing of the new ceramics is unlike the old process of molding and firing clay."

   Is this statement supported by information in the selection?

   ____

A TECHNICAL TRIUMPH

In November of 1984, United States and British scientists announced that they had succeeded in cloning the gene that causes blood to clot. The discovery has been called "a technical triumph without parallel" and a "staggering exploit." The blood-clotting gene was introduced by the scientists into a virus and then used to infect hamster kidney cells. The kidney cells of the hamster then made "Factor 8," the blood-clotting agent.

When a product in usable form is developed from this discovery, it will be prescribed for those who have hemophilia, an inherited disorder of the blood in which clotting does not occur normally. Because of this lack of clotting, a hemophiliac can bleed to death from internal injuries.

This blood disorder has been controlled thus far by frequent blood transfusions. These transfusions replace "Factor 8." A problem of transfusions to hemophiliacs is the possibility of contaminated blood supplies carrying the AIDS virus or hepatitis. AIDS affects the body's ability to fight infection and has caused a large number of deaths in recent years including the deaths of many who were infected through blood transfusions involving contaminated blood. Hepatitis is a virus which causes inflammation of the liver, fever, and usually jaundice (yellowness of the skin).

The need is for an effective, highly safe product that will bring relief to hemophiliacs.

QUESTIONS

1. Look closely at the first sentence in the second paragraph. What key word tells us that the author assumes a usable product for humans will develop from the experiment?

   a. When
   b. Form
   c. Discovery

2. Which of the following statements is supported by information from the story?

   a. To a hemophiliac, a small internal injury can be just as dangerous as a large cut to normal people.
   b. Hemophiliacs should avoid blood transfusions.
   c. Jaundice is always deadly for hemophiliacs.

3. The author says a hemophiliac can bleed to death from internal injuries. From what you know, is this a reasonable conclusion?

   ____

THE GREAT STORM OF 1913

A growing weather disturbance in Canada plus a low-pressure area from the southeast collided over the Great Lakes in November 1913. On Friday, November 7, the weather bureau issued storm warnings and hoisted warning flags. The Lake Carriers Association issued a bulletin which read in part: "No lake master can recall, in all his experience, a storm of such immense size, unusual violence, and rapid changes in the direction and speed of the winds." The waves were at least 35 feet high. The wind frequently blew in one direction, while the sea ran in the opposite direction.

One ship, the *L.C. Waldo,* with a cargo of iron ore, encountered towering waves that smashed the pilot house and steering wheel and drove the vessel onto a reef off the tip of Keweenaw Point. The *Waldo* broke in half. Somehow the crew survived for 90 hours in the forward end until they were rescued.

The barge *Plymouth* anchored near St. Martin's Island to ride out the storm. Icy waves broke over the barge but didn't sink it. The crew of seven lashed themselves to the rigging to keep from being swept overboard; they all froze to death. Besides several other instances like those described, there were some unexplained mysteries. Bodies of men from the ship *Charles S. Prince* washed up on the Ontario coast wearing life jackets from the ship *Regina.*

All in all, the great storm destroyed 19 ships, drove 20 more onto the rocks, drowned 250 seamen, and did millions of dollars worth of property damage. It is highly unlikely that a Great Lakes storm will ever cause such havoc again. Equipment is much improved. Hatch covers are stronger and almost impossible to tear open. Radio beacons give shipmasters a clear guide. Ship-to-shore communications provide up-to-date weather forecasting.

QUESTIONS

1. Which of the following conclusions is supported by information presented in the selection?

   a. The forward end of the *Waldo* sank after the storm.
   b. The forward end of the ship drifted out to sea.
   c. The forward end of the ship stayed afloat until the men were rescued.

2. What information does the selection present to support the conclusion that the storm was accompanied by cold temperatures?

____

3. Why were the bodies of the men from the *Prince* wearing life jackets from the *Regina?*

a. They stole them.
b. They were given them.
c. We don't know.

4. The author states that it is unlikely that a Great Lakes storm will ever cause such havoc again. Is it possible that the author is wrong? Why or why not?

____

____

3. Classifying Ideas, Objects, People, and Events

Classification is the process of grouping ideas, objects, people, and events according to the properties they have in common. It is much easier for us to understand the tremendous number of things in the world around us when we develop groupings of various kinds. If a friend mentions that he or she has a new tree in the backyard, you quickly form a mental image of the many kinds of trees you have seen in the past and you realize that this tree is likely to have certain physical characteristics in common with the other trees you have observed. It will probably be a living plant made of a woody fiber featuring roots, trunk, and limbs with leaves or needles. These are ***physical characteristics*** commonly associated with trees.

Trees may also be grouped with very different kinds of objects in a variety of ways. If you start with the heading *Sources of Building Materials,* you could group trees with sand, clay, various metals, rocks, etc. These materials do not look alike, but they serve people in a similar way. They are raw materials used in the construction of homes and other kinds of buildings. In this case, you are grouping objects according to their ***uses*** or ***common functions.*** You can group animals according to function, too. Some are sources of food; some help in transporting people and goods; some help guard other animals, homes, and businesses. In most cases, the parts of a large object are seen as having a common function. The roofs, rafters, walls, and windows of a building can be classified as serving a common function. The parts make the building possible. Without these parts, there would be no structure.

A third method of classification relates to the ***behavior*** of living and nonliving things. You may find that certain groups of animals breathe through their skins. Other creatures may move about using similar or identical means of locomotion. Scientists even refer to nonliving things as having ***common behaviors.*** Some materials will sink in water; others will float. Some materials will burn; others will not. We can, therefore, group materials that float or burn because they have these behaviors, or properties, in common.

Finally, you may group ideas, objects, people, and events by noting ***similarities of time and place.*** Historians, legal experts, anthropologists, and other people who are particularly interested in the past often associate ideas, people, objects, and events that happened at or about the same time or in the same regions of the world. They refer, for example, to the Bronze Age, the Pre-Civil War era, or the Post-Industrial Society. They also talk about people and events within regions — the Near Eastern Region, the Asian Subcontinent. Cultural traditions and happenings are often also grouped according to the geographical areas in which they took place. Combining time and place, historians can trace the development of ideas as they appeared, say, during the Golden Age of Greece or later in the Roman Empire.

1. Read over the groupings below and indicate in front of each one which kind of classification is being used. You have four choices:

Physical Characteristics	**Behavior**
Uses/Functions	**Time/Place**

The first one is done for you.

Uses/Functions a. Knife, fork, spoon, chopsticks.

____________ b. Ants, beetles, mosquitoes, and flies are insects.

____________ c. The War of 1812, the establishment of the National Bank, and the election of Andrew Jackson occurred before the Civil War.

____________ d. In the northern climate, the leaves drop from most trees as winter approaches.

____________ e. Robes, trousers, dresses, and long shirts of many designs and materials are worn by people for protection.

____________ f. Many animals have claws.

____________ g. These animals are all found in the Arctic regions.

____________ h. The run on the banks and the fall of the stock market occurred almost simultaneously.

____________ i. Hammers, screw drivers, saws, and sandpaper are needed to build a cabinet.

____________ j. Tents, apartments, cottages, and igloos serve people in much the same way.

____________ k. Allspice, pepper, nutmeg, cloves, and other seasonings should be kept on hand in the kitchen.

____________ l. Swords, bows and arrows, cannons, and slings have been used in warfare.

____________ m. The birds belonging to this family all have long beaks.

____________ n. The trigger, the barrel, and the bolt of the rifle are all needed for firing.

Answers:

b. Physical Characteristics
c. Time/Place
d. Behavior
e. Uses/Functions
f. Physical Characteristics
g. Time/Place
h. Time/Place
i. Uses/Functions
j. Uses/Functions
k. Uses/Functions
l. Uses/Functions
m. Physical Characteristics
n. Uses/Functions

2. Column I lists five categories or groups of animals. Column II lists some traits of each group. Match each set of traits with the correct group. Write the correct letter in the space in front of the animal category.

_______ Mammals	a. 3 pairs of legs; 3 main body parts; most have wings and antennae.
_______ Insects	b. Live in water; breathe through gills; cold-blooded.
_______ Reptiles	c. Young usually born alive and nurse; warm-blooded.
_______ Birds	d. Young usually hatched from eggs; cold-blooded.
_______ Fish	e. Young hatched from eggs; beaks; wings; warm-blooded.

Answers: c,a,d,e,b

3. The following animals can all be sorted into the five groups given above. Put each animal in the correct group.

hyena	***trout***	***lion***	***locust***	***mosquito***
cricket	***bee***	***robin***	***goat***	***lizard***
zebra	***hawk***	***snake***	***frog***	***flounder***
salmon	***toad***	***penguin***	***shark***	***parrot***

A. MAMMALS

____
____
____
____

B. INSECTS

____
____
____
____

C. REPTILES

____
____
____
____

D. BIRDS

____
____
____
____

E. FISH

____
____
____
____

Answers:
A. hyena, zebra, lion, goat
B. cricket, bee, locust, mosquito
C. toad, snake, frog, lizard
D. hawk, robin, penguin, parrot
E. salmon, trout, shark, flounder

4. People who work in business and industry often try to store their material in ways that will allow easy access. They must, however, use clearly defined categories.

Suppose, for the moment, that you work for a hamburger fast-food chain, and you have been assigned the job of putting items in proper storage areas. Read through the list of items in the box below and write each item under its proper heading.

hamburger patties, forks, broom, unopened jar of pickles, opened pickles, basket for making fries, cheese, unopened can of chocolate sauce, mop, ice cream, can of fruit, typewriter, milk, pencils, cleaning cloths, spoons, knife, cocoa mix, kitchen cleanser, typewriter paper, pie, drainer, floor cleaner, memo pads, electric mixer, unopened jar of jelly, disinfectant, rice, flour, powdered sugar, spaghetti

I. CUPBOARD FOR CANNED AND BOTTLED ITEMS

____
____
____
____

II. CANISTERS FOR DRY FOOD STORAGE

____
____
____
____
____

III. REFRIGERATOR AND FREEZER

____
____
____
____
____
____

IV. EATING UTENSILS AND COOKING EQUIPMENT

____
____
____
____
____
____

V. CLOSET FOR CLEANING SUPPLIES AND EQUIPMENT

____
____
____
____
____
____

VI. OFFICE SUPPLIES AND EQUIPMENT

____
____
____
____

Answers:

Group I.
jar pickles
can chocolate
can fruit
jar jelly

Group II.
cocoa mix
rice
flour
powdered sugar
spaghetti

Group III.
hamburger patties
opened pickles
cheese
ice cream
milk
pie

Group IV.
forks
basket for fries
spoons
knife
drainer
electric mixer

Group V.
broom
mop
cleanser
cleaning cloths
floor cleaner
disinfectant

Group VI.
typewriter
pencils
typewriter paper
memo pads

SHOES THROUGH THE AGES

At one time the kind of shoe you wore was determined by your rank in society. In ancient Egypt everyone wore sandals, but the sandals were of different kinds. Aristocrats wore sandals with pointed toes; sandals of common citizens were made of woven papyrus reeds; and slaves' sandals were made of palm leaves, a cheap material.

In Greece rich women had about 20 pairs of shoes. They took their shoes with them everywhere they went, but a slave carried the shoes. In Europe during the early Middle Ages, people wore a piece of untanned animal hide wrapped around the feet and tied with a thong.

Holland is known for its wooden shoes, but in the 1100's most poor Europeans wore them. These *sabots* were made of a single piece of wood. In England and Japan clogs made of fabric and mounted on wood blocks were popular.

Then a new fad became all the rage—pointed toes on shoes. The more pointed they became, the more fashionable they were. Finally, they got so long that they had to be stuffed with material to help keep the wearer from falling. Before the pointed-toe fad ran out, high heels became popular. In Venice, Italy, women wore platform shoes as high as stilts!

Henry VIII of England in the 16th century started a fashion for wide-toed shoes because he wanted to hide his gout, a condition that causes the toes to swell. Louis XIV of France in the 17th century wore high heels to make him look taller.

In the 1800's there arrived a great shoe development—the *last*. A last is a foot-shaped block of wood over which leather can be fitted and made into a shoe. For the first time in the long development of footwear, separate shoes could be made for the right and left feet!

Today shoes come in many types, styles, sizes, and prices. You may only want to spend a few dollars for sandals or perhaps you would prefer $7,000 for a mink-lined pair of shoes with 18-carat gold finish and ruby-tipped gold spikes!

QUESTIONS

1. Match the letter of each shoe type to the class of people who wore it.

________	Common Egyptian citizens.	a. Untanned animal hide tied with a thong.
________	Poor Europeans in the 1100's.	b. Sandals with pointed toes.
________	Egyptian slaves.	c. Sandals made of papyrus.
________	Europeans in the early Middle Ages.	d. Wooden sabots.
________	Ancient Egyptian aristocrats.	e. Sandals made of palm leaves.

2. Of the following items, which could ***not*** be classified as made partly of wood?

a. Sabots.
b. Egyptian sandals.
c. Lasts.

Each of the following groups contains four words. Only three of the items belong in the group. Circle the letter of the item that does ***not*** belong.

3. a. Sabots b. Clogs c. Lasts d. Sandals

4. a. Henry VIII b. Egyptian aristocrats c. Egyptian slaves d. Egyptian common citizens

5. The last paragraph of the story suggests four possible ways of classifying shoes: types, styles, sizes, and prices. Using the items in the box below, complete the outline. (Part of the outline has been done for you.)

wide widths	***laced***	***expensive***
athletic	***boots***	***pointed-toe***
bargain	***slippers***	***narrow widths***
open-toe	***buckled***	***oxford***
orthopedic		

I. TYPES
athletic
____
____
____
____

II. STYLES
open-toe
____
buckled
____

III. SIZES
wide widths
____

IV. PRICES
____
____

EDIBLE EXPLOSIONS

The Aztec Indians of Mexico used exploded kernels of corn to decorate their statues of the gods and to make elaborate headdresses. Further north, in what is now Massachusetts, an Indian named Quadequina in 1621 presented the Pilgrims, at their first Thanksgiving feast, with popped corn. Popped corn later became a token of good will and was often present at peace talks between Indians and Colonists.

The Indians believed a tiny demon resided inside each kernel of corn and made it pop.

The actual explanation is that when heated, the moisture inside the corn turns to steam. The hard outer covering doesn't let the steam escape, so it explodes.

There are four types of corn for popping. One is white. The other three are small-, medium-, and large-kernel yellow. Those who manufacture snacks favor the large-kernel yellow variety. These are used to make such confections as Cracker Jacks and popcorn flavored with chocolate or with watermelon or with many other flavors in between. New hybrid varieties have been developed over the years to yield much bigger kernels after popping. Hence those large, fluffy pieces. Much popcorn is machine picked, but a few of the most successful companies pick the corn by hand. They do not shell it immediately as machines do, but let it dry on the cob. It is shelled by a process that allows little contact of the corn with metal. Kernels are damaged by metal, and that is one of the two main reasons some kernels of corn do not pop. The other reason is lack of moisture.

The town of Van Buren, Indiana, is the popcorn Capital of the World. Every summer the town holds a three-day Popcorn Festival celebrating the much-loved snack. The United States is both the world's greatest grower of popcorn and its own best customer. According to the Popcorn Institute, Americans consume annually 42 quarts of popped corn for each man, woman, and child in the country. This makes popcorn a billion-dollar industry!

QUESTIONS

1. If you were the editor of a magazine, how would you classify this selection?

a. A fictional story about the first Thanksgiving.
b. A history of the production and uses of popcorn.
c. A biography of the Indian Quadequina.
d. A study of the religious ceremonies of the Aztecs.
e. A travel guide to Van Buren, Indiana.

2. White, small-kernel yellow, medium-kernel yellow, and large-kernel yellow are types of (what classification?)

____________________.

3. According to the article, how can Van Buren, Indiana, be classed with Rome, London, and Tokyo?

a. It is a large city.
b. It thinks of itself as a capital.
c. It holds a Popcorn Festival.

4. What classification of popcorn goes with "machine-picked"?

a. Hybrid.
b. Hand-picked.
c. Large-kernel.

INTELSAT

Intelsat is an organization of 109 member nations joined together to set up systems for the transmission and relay of voice, video, and data messages. The organization was begun in 1964. By 1965 it had 75 message circuits. It currently has about 500 times as many, a total of more than 37,000 in a 15-satellite network linked to 827 antennas at 658 ground stations around the world.

Intelsat's *Early Bird* satellite (Intelsat I, 1965) was made of aluminum and magnesium. It was just over two feet in diameter and less than two feet high. It was retired in 1969 because of the more powerful satellites then in orbit. The four Intelsat II series satellites were put in orbit in 1966 and 1967. They were also made of aluminum. They were almost five feet in diameter and just over two feet in height. They carried 240 two-way voice transmissions as well as television and teletype signals.

The Intelsat III satellites, deployed in 1968-1970, were also made of aluminum. Like the earlier satellites, these eight satellites were powered by solar cells and nickel-cadmium batteries. The capacity of the eight Intelsat IV satellites increased to 9,000 phone circuits and 12 color television broadcasts. Their size was nearly eight feet in diameter and nine feet high.

Intelsat has continued to send up even more powerful and efficient satellites. Earlier satellites were put into orbit by rockets, but later ones were taken up on the space shuttles and placed into orbit. Up until now, Intelsat has had a monopoly on this kind of transmission. However, within a few years, a competitive transmission system, Project TAT-8, the first trans-Atlantic fiber-optic cable, will be completed. It will be able to handle 37,000 voice, video, and data signals simultaneously.

QUESTIONS

1. When we classify things, we group them together according to qualities they share. What shared element allows us to place Intelsat II and Intelsat III in the same category?

a. Intelsat II and Intelsat III were the same size.
b. Intelsat II and Intelsat III were both launched at the same time.
c. Intelsat II and Intelsat III were both made of the same metal.

2. Which single characteristic was shared by all of the satellites?

a. They were all used for communication purposes.
b. They were all the same size.
c. They were all the same in capacity.

3. Which of the following is a characteristic of Intelsat's *Early Bird*?

a. Measurements of several hundred feet.
b. Aluminum and magnesium composition.
c. Launch date 1968.

4. Classify each of the satellites below by its size. Draw a line from the measurements on the left to the correct satellite on the right.

a. Diameter: 5 feet Height: 2 feet	Intelsat I
b. Diameter: 8 feet Height: 9 feet	Intelsat II
c. Diameter: 2 feet Height: 2 feet	Intelsat IV

5. You are a writer for a scientific journal. Given the information in this story, what are three ways you could classify the satellites in the Intelsat organization?

a. By series.
b. By weight.
c. By color.
d. By name.
e. By number of satellites in each series.
f. By orbit length.

6. Look through the list of characteristics in the box below. Write each characteristic under the correct satellite name.

240 two-way voice transmissions.	***9,000 phone circuits.***
"Early Bird."	***Retired in 1969.***
12 color television broadcasts.	***Deploy date 1966-1967.***
8 satellites.	***Deploy date 1968-1970.***

A. INTELSAT I
____
____

C. INTELSAT III
____
____

B. INTELSAT II
____
____

D. INTELSAT IV
____
____
____

4. Detecting Confusing Problems with Words

We have all heard humorous stories, jokes, and puns in which words can be interpreted in more than one way. A detective who likes soft drinks might say, for example, that he'd like to be assigned to the case of the reappearing root beer. We may find this humorous because detectives often work on cases, but in this situation the word *case* can also refer to the box in which the root beer is stored. When this detective works on the case of the reappearing root beer, he might have lots to drink.

There is also a story about a man who was trying to sell a race horse. He said that the horse was *fast in the mud*. The buyer who went to look at the horse found that it was, indeed, fast in the mud. The horse couldn't move its feet at all. All four of its hooves were firmly stuck in the wet dirt. In this case, "fast" could have two very different meanings. You might assume that the horse could move very rapidly. It was fast. It was a swift runner. You would be less likely to assume that the horse was stuck fast and couldn't move at all.

In the two situations described above, you will notice that the differences in meanings result from the fact that key words in the descriptions may be interpreted in very different ways. We call these *semantic problems*.

In addition to semantic problems, we have situations in which words are arranged in sentences in ways that make it difficult for the reader to know what the author is trying to tell us. Read the statement below.

> Susan and her mother went into a store,
> where she bought a dress.

The sentence doesn't really tell us which of the two people bought the dress, since the word "she" could refer to either Susan or her mother. This is called a *syntactical problem.* The statement below also illustrates this same problem.

> Ted often stays up late at night with
> a good book, in a colorful jacket.

We don't know whether the author is trying to tell us that Ted was dressed in a colorful jacket or that the book was covered in a colorful jacket.

If a statement can be interpreted in more than one way, we can't tell exactly what the author is trying to tell us. Two people reading the same sentence might have very different ideas regarding what it means.

Many of the following sentences contain some type of ambiguous meaning. Read the sentences carefully and then answer the questions. The first exercise is done for you.

1. Smoking cigarettes can cause fires.
What can cause fires?

a. Cigarettes that have been left smoking.
b. People smoking cigarettes.
c. Matches.
d. Can't tell.

The answer to the question above is ***d, can't tell,*** because it is not clear whether people smoking cigarettes cause fires or cigarettes that have been left smoking cause fires. The sentence can be interpreted either way.

2. A young woman carrying a small girl and her friend entered.
What was the young woman carrying?

a. A small girl.
b. A small girl and her friend.
c. A small girl and a friend of the small girl.
d. Can't tell.

3. His mother gave him a handsome boy's shirt.
Who or what was handsome?

a. The shirt.
b. The boy from whom the mother got the shirt.
c. Both the boy and the shirt.
d. Can't tell.

4. Each Sunday Bill visits the quiet little children's zoo.
What does Bill visit each Sunday?

a. A zoo for quiet little children.
b. A quiet little zoo for children.
c. A zoo where the animals make no noises.
d. Can't tell.

5. Tim and three other students were late for class.
How many students were late for class?

a. One.
b. Two.
c. Four.
d. Can't tell.

6. Would you rather that your father bawled you out or your older sister?
What does the question ask?

a. Who would you rather have bawl you out — your father or your older sister?
b. Who would you rather have your father bawl out — you or your older sister?
c. Would you rather be bawled out or not?
d. Can't tell.

7. Jane said, "I'll draw the curtains."
What was Jane going to do?

a. Close the curtains.
b. Draw a picture of the curtains.
c. Pull the curtains towards herself.
d. Can't tell.

8. The teacher said, "Billy, come up front for the present."
What was Billy to do?

a. Come up front for now.
b. Come up front for a gift.
c. Come get a present for someone else.
d. Can't tell.

9. Jack has a dog that smells better than people.
What does the sentence mean?

a. Jack's dog can detect odors better than people can detect odors.
b. Jack's dog has a better odor than people have.
c. Jack's dog can detect people better than people can detect him.
d. Can't tell.

10. The shooting of the hunters was terrible.
What was terrible?

a. The way the hunters shot.
b. The fact that the hunters were shot.
c. The thunderous noise that occurred when the hunters shot.
d. Can't tell.

11. They stood watching the fireworks in the backyard.
What did they do?

a. Watched fireworks going off in the sky as they stood in the backyard.
b. Watched fireworks going off in the backyard as they stood some place else.
c. Watched fireworks going off in the backyard while they stood in the backyard.
d. Can't tell.

12. George liked Mary better than Bob.
What does the sentence mean?

a. George liked Mary better than Bob liked Mary.
b. George liked Mary better than he liked Bob.
c. Bob liked Mary better than George liked Mary.
d. Can't tell.

13. Susan gives away quarters and whistles on the corner.
What does Susan give away?

a. Quarters.
b. Whistles.
c. Quarters and whistles.
d. Can't tell.

14. The drinking glass hit the window and it broke.
What broke?

a. The drinking glass.
b. The window.
c. Both the drinking glass and the window.
d. Can't tell.

15. The war poster urged: "Save grease and waste paper!"
What were the people urged to do?

a. Save grease and not save paper.
b. Save both grease and leftover waste paper.
c. Save their money when they work with grease and waste paper.
d. Can't tell.

16. The violinist was poor.
What does the sentence tell us about the violinist?
a. He couldn't play his violin very well.
b. He had very little money.
c. He was not feeling well.
d. Can't tell.

Answers: You should have chosen d, can't tell for all of the questions except number 5. The meaning of number 5 is clear (the answer is ***c. four***). All of the other sentences contain some type of ambiguous meaning.

Potentially confusing problems with words appear frequently in written material. But if a selection is well written, a careful reading of it will allow you to determine the author's intended meaning.

Read over the following paragraph from a selection about miniature horses. Pay attention to the two words in bold print to determine what meaning the author intended.

> The Sherman family of Hallsville, Texas, raises Appaloosa horses. The horses are tiny. None of ***them*** is more than three feet tall. They are only slightly larger than the family's Great Dane dog. Some years ago, the Shermans bought Chief. He was famous for fathering very small foals. Chief has since fathered 22 tiny horses. The Shermans keep ***these*** on their ranch in Hallsville.

17. What does "them" in the third sentence refer to?

a. The Shermans.
b. The miniature horses.

18. What does the "these" in the last sentence refer to?

a. Great Dane dogs.
b. 22 tiny horses.

The selection about miniature horses continues.

> Why do they raise miniature horses? Miniature horses make fine pets. They can easily be trained to pull a cart. They are so gentle that a three-year-old child can handle them ***while sitting in a cart.***

19. In the last sentence, whom does the author refer to as "sitting in a cart"?

a. Miniature horses.
b. Three-year-old child.

The selection continues.

> Miniature horses eat what other horses do, but ***they*** eat much less. A bale of hay lasts one of these tiny horses three months.
>
> At one time, miniatures had a hard life. They were used to haul coal in mines because they were small enough to move through the tunnels.
>
> You can hold a three-month-old foal on your lap. If a miniature horse doesn't go where you want, you just pick ***it*** up and put it there. Miniatures have recently been in great demand for horse shows, parades, and fairs.

20. In the first paragraph above, "they" refers to —

a. Miniature horses.
b. Other horses.

21. In the last paragraph, what do you "just pick up"?

a. Your lap.
b. The miniature horse.

Answers: 17. b, 18. b, 19. b, 20. a, 21. b. The context of the selection eliminates any ambiguity in these examples.

TALE OF UNBELIEVABLE DISASTERS

The wonder of the age, a ship five times larger than any other ship of her day, also proved to be the victim of several great disasters! The *Great Eastern* was 692 feet long, weighted 27,400 tons (that's 54,800,000 pounds), and carried 6,500 square yards of sail. She was planned by I.K. Brunel, who had built a tunnel under the Thames River in England earlier.

On November 3, 1857, as 125,000 persons watched, tugs, winches, and hydraulic rams strained to launch the ship sideways (a first). The ship budged *three inches!* On another try, a windlass spun violently. Two workers were thrown into the air and killed. Finally, the ship set off for America. Shortly afterwards, a giant explosion blew off the forward funnel and started fires. Five persons died.

In 1860 the ship again set off for the United States. This time she landed in New York with a bang, crushing five feet of the wharf. Still, 2,000 people bought tickets for a two-day cruise. First, there was not enough food. Next, 1,700 people had to sleep on the deck in the rain. To top it off, the ship got lost and sailed 100 miles off course.

Later, the *Great Eastern* sailed from Halifax, Nova Scotia, to England in nine days and four hours — a record voyage! But on the return trip she ripped a huge hole in her hull near Long Island. Nevertheless, Napoleon III, the Emperor of France, wanted to use the ship to bring wealthy Americans to France for the Universal Exhibition. The *Great Eastern* was elegantly refitted. On the way to pick up the passengers, she ran into a cyclone.

Finally, the *Great Eastern* was sold for $80,000 (she had cost five million dollars). In 1889 the ship was broken up.

QUESTIONS

1. Who is the "she" in paragraph 1?

a. I.K. Brunel.
b. The ship.
c. A lady on the ship.

2. In the second sentence in paragraph 3, what does the author mean by saying the ship "landed with a bang"?

a. The ship had an accident.
b. The ship shot its guns.
c. The ship was successful.

3. In the same sentence, what does the word "feet" refer to?

a. Bottom supports.
b. Units of length.

4. In the last sentence in paragraph 3, what does the word "course" mean?

a. Class in school.
b. Direction.
c. Part of a meal.

5. In the last paragraph, what do the words "broken up" mean?

a. Emotionally upset.
b. Stopped.
c. Taken apart.

HOLDING THINGS TOGETHER

About 20,000 B.C. a most important question was: How could one fasten an animal hide around the body without having to hold it with one hand? There were these choices: Use thorns or fishbones; or poke holes in the skin and tie the parts together with a long, thin piece of hide. The thorn-fishbone solution led to pins (from the Latin *spina*, meaning "thorns"); the second choice brought about needles (to pull the pieces of hide). By the end of the Ice Age, bone needles had progressed to the point of having eyes.

After metal needles came along, someone got the bright idea of doubling the wire, then bending one end so the other end fit in it. Graves scattered from Greece to Denmark belonging to the Late Bronze Age are full of these ancient safety pins, some complete with a springlike circle such as the one that creates tension in modern safety pins. Ancient Greece and Rome changed these humble pins into ornate brooches, used both to fasten robes and mantles and to show the wealth of the owners.

The straight pin was used by women in ancient Athens to bind their chitons (tunics or loose-fitting garments). In the 14th century in Europe straight pins were in such great demand that one French princess had 12,000 of them, while in England a special tax was levied to keep the queen in pins. Ordinary persons could buy pins only on January first and second. Ladies set aside money for this pilgrimage and called it, appropriately, "pin money."

As efficient as the safety pins were, it is strange that the idea of them got lost and had to be re-invented. Walter Hunt, a Quaker in New York, owed money and found a way to repay it. In three hours time he twisted up a "safety" pin and sold the patent rights to pay his debt! The coil at one end was not new, as examples from the Bronze Age attest.

QUESTIONS

1. If you had not read the story, what might you think the title means? (Choose three.)

a. The uses of a crowbar.
b. The uses of glue.
c. How to tie different kinds of knots.
d. The separation of the North and South before the Civil War.

e. How to pull the foil off a chewing gum wrapper.
f. The history and production of paper clips.

2. "How could one fasten an animal hide around the body without having to hold *it* with one hand?"
What does "it" refer to?

a. The body.
b. The hand.
c. The hide.

3. "The thorn-fishbone solution led to pins; the *second choice* brought about needles."
What does the "second choice" refer to?

a. Fishbones.
b. Thin pieces of hide.
c. The process of poking holes in the skin and pulling thin pieces of hide through the holes.

4. "*Ordinary persons* could buy pins only on January first and second."
What does "ordinary persons" refer to?

a. People who were boring.
b. People who weren't crazy.
c. People who were not royalty.

5. "Ladies set aside money for this pilgrimage and called *it* 'pin money'."
What does the "it" in this sentence refer to?

a. Their pilgrimage.
b. Their money.
c. Their pins.

6. "In England, a special tax was levied to keep the queen in pins."
In this sentence, the author means –

a. The special tax money was used to buy plenty of pins for the queen.
b. The special tax money was pinned onto the queen.
c. The special tax money made the queen nervous.

In each of the sentences below, decide what meaning of the word in italics makes sense in the sentence.

7. "Bone needles progressed to the point of having *eyes*."

a. Organs for seeing.
b. Openings for thread.

8. "The skin was tied together with pieces of *hide*."

a. Conceal.
b. Animal skin.

9. "Romans used pins to fasten their robes and *mantles*."

a. Coats.
b. Fireplaces.

EYEGLASSES

It is difficult for people in the modern age to envision a world without eyeglasses. But the Dark Ages were dim and fuzzy for many people. Medieval men and women with seeing problems had to rely on folk medicine cures. One Anglo-Saxon remedy advised people with poor vision to comb their heads, eat little meat, and drink wormwood before meals — or to apply a salve made from nuts, salt, and wine to their eyes.

In the 4th century, people believed that a person seeing a falling star should quickly begin counting. The viewer would be free from eye inflammations for as many years as he or she counted before the star disappeared. There were other equally useless beliefs.

An 11th-century Arab study mentioned the idea of corrective lenses, but there is no evidence that the idea had yet been put into practice. During the 13th century, vision defects began to be taken more seriously. When spectacles began to appear around Pisa late in the 1280's, the lenses were convex. These were only good for far-sighted people. They were used to help in reading. They didn't become very popular because few people could read.

The earliest optical lenses were made of the transparent minerals beryl or quartz and set in frames of brass or iron and later in bone, horn, gold, or leather. Some early spectacles were held on the nose by a hook affixed to a cap. Only the very wealthy could afford these early eyeglasses. But by 1500 spectacles had become cheap enough for a wider part of the population to afford. In the 16th century lenses for near-sighted people were invented. Persons who wanted spectacles stopped by a shop and tried on glasses until a pair was found that was helpful. In the late 18th century side pieces, or bows, were first used.

By the 1870's trained vision specialists fitted glasses, though some Americans still bought their eyeglasses from mail-order houses as late as 1960. The 20th century marked the first time that eyeglasses were fashionable.

Contact lenses became useful to many people in about 1950. These lenses fit the cornea rather than the whole eye. Special types of glasses for many needs are available today.

QUESTIONS

In each statement below, the word in italics can have more than one meaning. Read the statement and then look closely at the two sentences below it. Decide which of these two sentences uses the word in much the same way as in the sentence from the selection.

1. "One Anglo-Saxon remedy advised people with *poor* vision to comb their heads."

a. The poor man begged for money.
b. Your poor grades will get you kicked off the team.

2. "Another remedy advised people to eat *little* meat."

a. You seem to care little about your bad behavior.
b. My swimsuit is too little.

3. "The *viewer* of a falling star could discover the number of years he or she would be free of eye trouble."

a. Television viewers ultimately determine what programs appear on prime time.
b. Drop the slide into a slot on top and point the viewer toward a bright light.

4. "An Arab *study* mentioned corrective lenses."

a. Myra planned to study after basketball practice.
b. Several studies have linked cigarette smoking to cancer.
c. Even though he was sick, Dan asked his sister to bring home his books because he didn't want to fall behind in his studies.

5. "Eleventh-century corrective lenses did not improve *vision*."

a. The bus driver's vision was impaired because of the thick fog.
b. The prophet claimed she had had a vision about the future.

6. "*Spectacles* in the late 1280's had convex lenses."

a. Jessica was delighted to trade in her spectacles for a pair of contact lenses.
b. The spectacle of Brian dressed in a chicken suit delighted everyone at the party.

7. "Early optical lenses were set in different types of *frames*."

a. Mom wanted matching frames for our baby pictures.
b. My score was so lousy that I gave up bowling after three frames.
c. Both accused smugglers claimed their arrests were actually frames.

8. "Early frames were made of bone, *horn*, or leather."

a. Jazz great Louis Armstrong sang and played his horn for thousands of fans.
b. Even the best matador never knows when he will be gored by the bull's horns.

5. Selecting Criteria for Use in Making Judgments

When you select criteria to use in making decisions, you develop or choose standards. These standards help you decide on the value or worth of something or somebody. Let's assume, for example, that you want to buy a ten-speed bike. You might decide that you want one that is inexpensive, lightweight, and durable (well made) and has a front wheel that can be easily removed. As you go from one bicycle store to the next, you examine bikes to see if they have the characteristics you value. This is an intelligent way to make decisions. Otherwise, you might just choose a flashy bike and find out later that it really doesn't suit your needs.

Criteria are also useful in judging people. A group of upper elementary students were recently arguing about which of our American leaders and scientists were the greatest or most important. The discussion seemed to go on endlessly until one bright young lady suggested that they develop a list of standards (criteria) and rate each leader and scientist on each standard. After the criteria were agreed upon, the rating of the leaders went rather smoothly.

1. Let's assume that you are going to select a new player for your softball team. You need someone who is especially good because your team is at the bottom of the league. Which *five* of the characteristics listed below do you think would be most important?

a. The ability to read baseball instructions in books.
b. Skill in throwing and catching the ball.
c. A happy home.
d. The ability to get along with other players.
e. Batting skills.
f. Speed in running bases.
g. Pride in taking care of a uniform.
h. Willingness to take directions from the coach.
i. Good manners and good sportsmanship.
j. Skill in keeping accurate team records.
k. Willingness to try hard in practices and league games.
l. Skill in fielding the ball.

Answers: Not everyone will pick the same criteria, but you should at least have included b, e, f, and l.

POON LIM'S RECORD

Poon Lim holds the world's record for surviving on an ocean raft. He floated alone for 133 days with little food and water. His comment about his trip was, "I hope no one will ever have to break my record."

Poon Lim was a Chinese sailor aboard the steamship *Ben Lomond.* On November 22, 1942, during World War 2, the boat was sunk by a German submarine soon after leaving Cape Town, South Africa. Poon Lim put on a life jacket and jumped into the water. For two hours he floated, hoping to spot a life raft from the sinking ship. Finally he found one. He climbed onto it and checked out the supplies. Some tins of biscuits were tied to it. There were also a water jug and a few flares.

Soon the food and water were almost gone. Poon Lim decided to catch rainwater in the covering of his life jacket. Next, he got a piece of wire from one of the flares. With this, he made a fishhook and caught several fish.

At the end of the second month he spotted sea gulls. For bait he used some of his precious fish. Soon Poon Lim captured a gull. But in the process he received deep cuts from the bird's beak and claws.

Some time after that he caught a small shark. The shark attacked after Poon Lim pulled it aboard the raft. Poon Lim hit it on the head with the water jug. He let some of the shark meat dry for use later on.

Poon Lim counted the days with notches on the side of the raft. On the 131st day he noticed the ocean water had turned pale green. Many birds flew overhead. On the morning of the 133rd day he saw a small sail. He waved his shirt to get the attention of the men on the boat. They changed course and came towards him.

Poon Lim received many honors. Congress invited him to come and live in the United States. He accepted and has remained here ever since.

QUESTIONS

1. If you were deciding what kind of person might be able to beat Poon's record, what characteristics would you look for? Select three.

   a. Good health.
   b. Knowledge of the sea.
   c. Many friends.
   d. Intelligence and cleverness.
   e. Patience.
   f. Kindness to animals.
   g. A good reader.

2. In describing Poon Lim and his experiences the selection emphasizes one particularly important characteristic that helps to explain Poon's survival. What is this characteristic?

a. His Chinese background.
b. The fact that he was from the steamship *Ben Lomond.*
c. His resourcefulness.

A DOG'S LIFE

For thousands of years human beings have enjoyed the companionship of dogs. Back in the Ice Ages primitive people began to tame wild dogs. Before recorded history people had even begun to breed types of dogs. Some of the early breeds were joined to get specific characteristics, such as skill at herding animals and scenting game.

Today the American Kennel Club divides the various breeds of dogs into six categories: working dogs, sporting dogs, hounds, nonsporting dogs, terriers, and toys. Sheep-herding collies and Alaskan malamutes belong in the working class. The sporting hounds track their quarry through rivers and woods. Terriers and such nonsporting dogs as poodles are familiar pets. And tiny toy dogs allow people in cramped quarters to own pets.

Whatever the breed, dogs share some common characteristics, such as a keen sense of smell and loyalty to their human masters.

QUESTIONS

1. Imagine now that you are the owner of a large kennel. You have several customers who want different types of dogs. Using the criteria at the left, match each customer with a kind of dog on the right.

_____ A woman who lives in an apartment wants a pet.
_____ A farm family wants a dog to help with the livestock.
_____ A man asks you for a dog to be his companion. The man enjoys duck hunting.
_____ The police captain wants a dog to help track down an escapee.
_____ A forest ranger calls to request a dog to help locate a lost camper.
_____ A rancher who raises sheep wants a working dog for her ranch.

a. Golden retriever
b. Bloodhound
c. Toy poodle
d. Collie

THE LONGEST RACE IN HISTORY

On March 4, 1926, a field of 199 men toed a starting line in Los Angeles. The starter's pistol cracked, and the runners were off in a cloud of dust on the longest marathon race ever run. The runners had to pay an entry fee of $100 for the privilege of running 3,422 miles to Madison Square Garden in New York City. Each had a chance of winning part of $48,500 in prizes, $25,000 of which was to go to the winner.

The runners completed a specified distance each day. Their running times were recorded, and the runner with the lowest accumulated times was to be declared the winner. At the end of the first day 76 runners had already dropped out. The survivors continued across the deserts of Arizona and New Mexico and up through the Texas Panhandle to Oklahoma, Missouri, and Illinois. By the time the runners reached Ohio, only 55 remained in the race.

The winner was Rudy Payne, 17, a part-Cherokee Indian. He covered the distance in 573 hours, four minutes, and 34 seconds, finishing a full 15 hours ahead of the runner-up. He had averaged a speed of six miles per hour in the longest foot race in history!

QUESTIONS

1. If you were comparing the achievement of Rudy Payne to the achievements of other marathon runners, what characteristics of Payne's race would you select as particularly important? One criterion might be the length of the race. List three others.

a. ______________________________

b. ______________________________

c. ______________________________

2. What are some of the important criteria that characterize the way this particular race was organized? One criterion might be the amount of the prize money. List three others.

a. ______________________________

b. ______________________________

c. ______________________________

6. Figurative Language

Figurative language refers to a writer's or speaker's use of words to create visual pictures in the minds of readers and listeners. This section will focus on three kinds of figurative language:

1. Simile
2. Hyperbole
3. Personification

Similes are used frequently by writers. They are used to draw comparisons of *un*like things — people, objects, places, or events. A simile usually makes use of the words *like* or *as* to form these comparisons. A person describing an intelligent friend might say, "She's as sharp as a tack." Another individual might describe a fast runner by saying, "He goes like the wind!" Notice that these comparisons are exaggerations. If we simply say that a wolf is like a dog, we are not using a simile. In this case, the listener is being asked to take the information literally.

1. Pick out the five similes in the sentences below.

a. Mary liked the game very much.
b. Tim fought like a tiger.
c. Matt ran around the store like a madman.
d. A horse is somewhat like a cow.
e. Sarah was as happy as a lark.
f. The car came by as he crossed the street.
g. Jim felt like a million dollars.
h. Rosa was as stubborn as a mule.

Answers: Did you put checks beside b, c, e, g, and h?

Hyperbole also involves the use of exaggerations: "I'm so proud, I could burst!" "I'm so ashamed, I could die!" "I'm so hungry, I could eat a horse!" Nobody really believes that you will burst, die, or eat a horse. But the use of hyperbole adds color, interest, and intensity to your comments. Sometimes hyperbole is used to make a point stronger. It calls attention to your idea. It is also more likely to be remembered by listeners.

Occasionally, hyperbole is used sarcastically to point out the traits of another person, such as laziness or tardiness. In jest, we may say that the lazy worker works her fingers to the bone. Or we may say that the tardy worker is standing at the factory entrance hours before the gate opens.

2. Pick out the five examples of hyperbole in the sentences below.

a. When Terry tore her dress, she screamed, "My mother will kill me!"
b. When it was Mary's turn to speak, she said she thought she would fall through the floor.
c. José worried that his uncle might have a heart attack.
d. Tim felt he'd rather die than confess that he was late again.
e. Sally said she was up to her ears in homework.
f. Al said that he was breaking his back from morning to night, but that he had little to show for his efforts.
g. Cindy almost broke her arm trying to crawl out the window.
h. The rapids were dangerous. They could pull you under in seconds.

Answers: Did you put checks beside a, b, d, e, and f?

Personification is the tendency we have to attribute human characteristics to other living and nonliving objects we encounter in the world. We may speak of an ocean liner as though it has feelings and a mind of its own. We may refer to the wind, the streams, and the clouds as if they also have personal qualities. Writers often describe the great forces of nature as though they were beings with human impulses, cares, and dislikes. They say that the river is rampaging, the winds are sighing, the lightning is fierce, and the mountains fall abruptly to the ocean.

3. Pick out the five examples of personification in the sentences below.

a. The ocean roared as the wind picked up.
b. Tom worked like a beaver.
c. The wind screamed, and the tree branches tore at their clothes.
d. Ralph was worried and really on edge.
e. The wind's icy fingers made them wish they had not started out.
f. Bret's hair was standing on end.
g. Tom could hear the rain beating on the window panes.
h. The sea was stubborn. It wouldn't give up its treasures of fish.

Answers: Did you put checks beside a, c, e, g, and h?

The story below has similes, an example of hyperbole, and a few illustrations of personification in it.

SHE FELL SIX MILES

Boom! There was an explosion high in the air. A Yugoslav DC-9 on a regular flight from Stockholm to Belgrade was ripped apart like an egg carton. Wreckage and bodies were flung by invisible hands toward the earth like matchsticks.

The tail section raced down through the clouds and plunged into a snowy wooded slope. A game warden named Henke reached the wreckage first. He heard a feeble moan, like the cry of a newborn baby. Vesna Valovic, a 23-year-old stewardess on the plane, was lying in the snow.

Henke covered her with his coat and hurried to get help. An ambulance rushed her to a hospital, where she underwent a three-hour operation.

Vesna regained consciousness. She even remembered her name and flight number. The doctor who had operated on her conferred with another surgeon, and Vesna was transferred by helicopter to Prague for neurosurgery. In Prague, specialists removed a section of vertebra pressing on her spinal cord. Vesna recovered slowly, but she remembered nothing of the fall. It was as though it had never happened. She did remember the explosion. She said she felt as though her heart had dropped to her feet.

Why did Vesna survive when no one else did? Evidence shows that she was about to serve a meal. She was standing in the aisle and was able to grab an oxygen mask. This provided her with oxygen during the fall.

When the tail section broke off, Vesna was thrown like a pillow into a corner. Knocked unconscious, she was relaxed during the fall. Tree branches reached out and cushioned the impact of her fall. Vesna was thrown clear, sliding down a hill, further reducing the jarring fall. Vesna, the girl who fell six miles, is listed in medical history as an incredible example of the durability of the human body.

QUESTIONS

1. Which of the following sentences contains an example of hyperbole?

   a. She felt as though her heart had dropped to her feet.
   b. She is listed in medical history as an incredible example of the durability of the human body.

2. Which of the following sentences contains a simile?

   a. He heard a moan, like the cry of a newborn baby.
   b. Why did Vesna survive when no one else did?

3. Which of the following sentences contains personification?

   a. Bodies were flung by invisible hands toward the earth.
   b. It was as though it had never happened.

4. Put an ***S*** in front of each phrase or sentence that contains a simile and a ***P*** if it contains personification.

_____ Bodies like matchsticks.
_____ The tail section raced through the clouds.
_____ The plane was ripped apart like an egg carton.
_____ Thrown like a pillow.
_____ Tree branches reached out.

GLORY, DEFEAT, GLORY AGAIN

In 1978 a young jockey, just 18 years old, took the horse-racing world by storm. Steve Cauthen, riding the horse Affirmed — and riding like the wind — won not only the Kentucky Derby, but also the Preakness and the Belmont Stakes. This gave him the Triple Crown of racing, an honor rarely won, and the supreme goal of jockeys. Having hit the top at the beginning of his career, what was left for him to accomplish?

Fate did not continue to favor "The Kid," as he was admiringly known. That same summer, he suffered knee and shoulder injuries in a spill at Saratoga Race Track. When he returned, some owners and trainers seemed to have lost faith in him. The autumn season was rough. The winter, in California, was devastating. He lost 110 races!

At this point, fate again intervened. Robert Sangster, a wealthy man who was well known in international racing, asked Steve to ride for him in England. Sangster was surprised and pleased when Steve agreed. And as for Steve, he found English and European racing seemed to smile on him.

In Europe all Steve has done is win. Steve now has a five-foot high silver trophy. He is the first American to win the jockey championship in Great Britain since 1913 and the youngest one to accomplish it since 1846!

"Some people wrote me off at 18," Steve said. Yet he has proved that after empty days, there can always be another dream, and a way to make it come true.

QUESTIONS

1. "Steve Cauthen took the horse-racing world by storm." This sentence is an example of —

   a. Hyperbole
   b. Personification
   c. Simile

2. Which of the following statements is a simile?

   a. The autumn was rough for Cauthen.

b. In Europe all he has done is win.
c. Cauthen rode like the wind.

3. "At this point, fate again intervened," is an example of —

a. Hyperbole
b. Personification
c. Simile

4. Of the two statements below, which contains personification?

a. Some people wrote Cauthen off at 18.
b. European racing seemed to smile on him.

WAGING WAR ON SOUTHERN MOSQUITOES

The southern mosquito has been called "a five-pound bug that bites like a rattler and buzzes like a B-52." Thus it isn't surprising that a "swat team" is going after the creatures. The Texas species of the mosquito has been known to swarm in dense funnels 300 feet high, blackening the sky. In a single four-inch by six-inch bag, 10,000 mosquitoes have been captured in one try!

Jim Olson studies the mosquito in wetlands from California to the Gulf Coast, where there are heavy concentrations. Mosquitoes breed in fields, then migrate to the cities, attracted by lights. In temperate climates, there are summertime species that die in winter, and winter species that die in summer.

The nastiest and most annoying is a dark, rice-field mosquito, which originated in Colombia, South America. These insects hatch in warm floodwater; thus rice paddies are perfect breeding grounds. Once they have bred, there are plenty of meals available in the Sun Belt cities. The number two demon is a standing-water breeder. It carries the disease St. Louis encephalitis. This one also makes duck and goose hunting miserable. Number three is the malaria carrier, sometimes known as the "four-spot" mosquito.

Pesticides alone do not eliminate mosquitoes, so other methods to get rid of them have been devised. The most powerful of these consists of the poisonous droppings of a bacteria found in the soil of Israel. This substance is added to the water when larvae are developing. The larvae are "blown apart" by the substance. This particular kind of bacteria does not hurt humans or useful insects which eat mosquitoes.

Olson is also experimenting with a back-swimming bug, and a beetle with an appetite as large as a horse, as well as an African fish which is put in storage tanks when rice fields are drained and then released when the new paddies are filled. All of these animals feed on mosquitoes and their larvae.

As part of his research, Jim has also come up with his own clever invention. It is "a remote-control bug net on wings with a tiny motor." This instrument flies to the top of the swarms and plucks out a few females. The sample allows the scientists to learn how these huge swarms migrate and breed.

QUESTIONS

1. Place an ***H*** in front of each sentence that contains hyperbole, a ***P*** if it contains personification, and an ***S*** if it contains a simile.

_____ a. The southern mosquito bites like a rattler.
_____ b. The bugs blacken the sky.
_____ c. The dark, rice-field mosquito is nasty and ill tempered.
_____ d. The number-two demon is a standing-water breeder.
_____ e. The larvae are "blown apart" by the substance.
_____ f. A beetle has an appetite as large as a horse.
_____ g. The remote-control bug net plucks out female mosquitoes.

7. Problems with Generalizations

When Bill Jenkins visited Florida in August, he suffered from unrelenting summer heat. He sought relief on the beaches, but the hot sand burned his feet and the scorching sun blistered his shoulders. After his return to his home in Maine, Bill shared his thoughts regarding Florida weather with his friends. He decided that Florida was not a very pleasant place to live. His limited acquaintance with the state led him to some very firm conclusions regarding the climatic conditions in that region of the country.

It must have been apparent to those who heard Bill's unflattering comments that he was drawing conclusions on the basis of very limited experiences in the state. He was totally unacquainted with Florida weather during other seasons of the year. In fact, he could not even be certain that the August temperatures he experienced were typical of August readings recorded for other years.

Bill Jenkins is not alone in his tendency to jump to conclusions. We all do it. Because of the pressures of time, we are often forced to make hasty generalizations. We encounter so many people, places, and events in the course of a week that we could not possibly know much about any one of these rapidly occurring experiences. They are often recorded in our minds as fleeting impressions. They are hastily collected, untested generalized feelings that often prove to be inaccurate or incomplete upon further examination.

We should be very careful when we come up with a generalization. Is it too sweeping? Have we stated it in a way which does not allow for any exceptions? Have we looked at enough of the facts? Have we come up with a statement which sets forth a fixed and unwavering truth, whereas the facts of the matter only support a tendency, something that is usually the case, but not always?

In particular, we should be sensitive to the crucial role of highly exclusive words. Whenever we use rigid remarks, such as "nobody," "everyone," "no one," "always," "never," "all," and "none," we are asking for trouble. These intractable words are very limiting. They often close the door to further inquiry and block competing views and interpretations. It is wiser in many circumstances to use such words as "sometimes results," "is related," "influences," or "in most periods" when you offer generalizations. Words like these leave the door open to further discussion, and our generalizations often need to be open to modification and correction.

1. From the eight generalizations below, pick out six that use highly exclusive, rigid words.

a. People who live on farms are never able to adjust fully to city life.
b. Nobody will ever run for the U.S. Senate without a large public backing.
c. People without much ambition always seen to end up in the poor house.
d. The United States will never yield to terrorists.
e. Poverty seems to contribute to the growth of crime.
f. Recent studies indicate that people can break the smoking habit when public efforts are made to convince them of the dangers involved.

g. Everybody in the South seems to think that Northerners are not honest.
h. Bountiful crops have always been a blessing to humanity.

Answers: Did you select a, b, c, d, g, and h? These generalizations all use highly exclusive, rigid words.

2. From the next eight generalizations, pick out five which avoid the problem of being too sweeping and too limiting, and which therefore allow for exceptions and the possibility of change.

a. The utilization of natural resources is related to the desires of human beings and the level of technology in human society.
b. Competition for the earth's natural resources sometimes results in political strife and even war.
c. Human society will always need to use oil as a source of energy.
d. The races, cultures, and civilizations in most areas of the world and in most historical periods have made some contributions to the growth of our present civilizations.
e. Machines are the enemy of the working person.
f. Much of civilization's progress can be traced to people's search for a larger measure of personal freedoms.
g. The culture within which people are reared exerts a powerful influence on them throughout their lives.
h. Milk has been and always will be the primary food for human babies.

Answers: Did you select a, b, d, f, and g? The others (c, e, and h) are too sweeping.

SKIING OVER BACTERIA

During the winter of 1984-85, billions of dead bacteria were used on ski slopes in a new ice-making project. This system had been successfully tested for the three preceding winters. The bacteria were mixed with water, added to compressed air, and sent out of the nozzles of snow-making machines. As the bacteria fell to the ground through the freezing air, they were encased in the ice crystals.

The bacteria are prepared by being shot with gamma rays (which kill them) and then freeze dried. These bacteria, alive or dead, are harmless to humans. They are found in the air and growing on the undersides of the leaves of most species of plants in temperate regions. When the bacteria on a plant form frost, they cause the plant to release chemicals to repair the frost damage. The bacteria live on these chemicals.

The purpose of using the bacteria is to allow snow to be made at warmer temperatures. Most snow-making operations need a temperature of 17 degrees Fahrenheit, while the bacteria-added system can operate at 20 degrees. In addition, the bacteria increase the volume of snow in relation to the volume of air and water.

Although water freezes at 32 degrees Fahrenheit, lower temperatures are needed for pure ice. At temperatures just under 32 degrees, crystals form only around something solid. In nature, snowflakes and ice crystals form around dust particles in the air. Ski areas also use silver iodide as particles for making snow. This is better than dust but requires lower temperatures than bacteria.

"Snowmax," as the system is called, allows snowmakers to turn out more snow with less energy. It can be used with the same snowmakers that are already in use. More slopes can be covered earlier in the season. Snowmax can also be used to increase the speed of freezing such food products as popsicles and ice cream.

QUESTIONS

1. In each of the generalizations below, underline the word that is highly exclusive or rigid.

   a. All ski slopes use bacteria to make ice.
   b. This type of bacteria is never harmful to people.
   c. Ski resorts always need new ways to produce artificial snow.
   d. Nobody prefers artificial snow over real snow.
   e. Every snow-making operation needs a temperature between 16 and 18 degrees.
   f. Only professional skiers enjoy snow made by "Snowmax."
   g. Scientists always tamper with nature.
   h. No scientist will ever be able to use Snowmax to change the weather.
   i. Food products should never contain chemicals.
   j. Bacteria are the only producers of artificial snow.

A CONTINUING LOVE AFFAIR

In 1700 Governor William Bladen of Maryland wrote, ". . . we had dessert no less Curious, among the Rarities of which it was Compos'd was some fine Ice Cream which, with strawberries and Milk, eat most deliciously." By the time of the Revolution, ice cream was sold in exclusive New York confectionery shops. George Washington liked ice cream so much that in the summer of 1790 he bought about $200 worth from a New York City ice cream merchant. Thomas Jefferson was as inventive with ice cream as he was with other things. He had his own 18-step recipe for making ice cream and a unique method of serving it — in balls inside warm pastry. He also introduced to America its favorite flavor when he brought 200 vanilla beans and a recipe for vanilla ice cream back from France. Dolley Madison preferred strawberry ice cream, which she served mounded in a "large shining dome" on a silver platter.

Earlier, in the 13th century, Marco Polo had in his travels to the Far East learned of a recipe for a frozen dessert made with milk. He brought the recipe with him when he returned to Italy. From there, in the 16th and 17th centuries, the idea of the frozen milk dessert spread across Europe.

The first of these desserts were ices and sherbets. Eventually, confectioners began as well to make the much richer ice cream. When ice cream became more widely available in the late 1800's, ice cream parlors began appearing in Europe and in all the major American cities.

In 1846 Nancy Johnson invented the hand-cranked ice cream freezer. In 1851 Jacob Fussell became the first full-fledged ice cream manufacturer and wholesaler in America. Robert Green is generally acknowledged to be the inventor of the ice cream soda. He was running a soft-drink stand at the Franklin Institute in Philadelphia in 1874. When he ran out of cream for a drink he made, he substituted ice cream.

New frozen products pop up from time to time, but ice cream continues to remain popular. Americans currently produce 8,500 million gallons of ice cream per year, enough for several single-scoop cones for every human being on earth.

QUESTIONS

Below are several generalizations relating to the information presented in the story. In each pair of sentences, one is a valid statement and one is a hasty generalization. Select the hasty generalization.

1. a. George Washington bought a large amount of ice cream.
b. Our early leaders spent money foolishly.

2. a. Some of the new uses for ice cream were discovered by accident.
b. Experiments with ice cream are always successful.

3. a. Thomas Jefferson developed an ice cream recipe.
b. Thomas Jefferson loved to cook.

4. a. Americans eat too much ice cream.
b. American are big consumers of ice cream.

5. a. Vanilla is America's favorite ice cream flavor.
b. Everybody loves vanilla ice cream.

6. a. The wives of early Presidents served food in strange ways.
b. Dolley Madison served ice cream mounded in a shining dome.

7. a. Ice cream parlors developed when ice cream became more available.
b. People preferred eating ice cream in parlors instead of at home.

8. a. Marco Polo introduced a recipe for ice cream to Italy.
b. If Marco Polo had not brought a recipe from the Far East, Europeans would never have known about ice cream.

"BAT" MASTERSON

William Masterson was a famous Western lawman. But when he was sheriff of Ford County, Kansas, in the 1870's, his favorite weapon was a cane!

Masterson's reputation as a tough but peace-loving enforcement officer began when he used a six-gun to collect wages from a contractor for the Santa Fe railroad. His reputation grew with stories about his skill and daring as a buffalo hunter. Then in 1872 he and 27 others repelled an attack by 500 Comanche, Kiowa, and Cheyenne Indians.

After Masterson became sheriff in Ford County, the cane became his trademark and earned him the nickname "Bat." Without a shot being fired, he captured the outlaw Dave Rudabaugh and his gang of bank robbers. Masterson disliked killing and violence. He avoided gun play, but he kept his shooting skills sharp and ready. He called gun practice "sweetening his gun."

While he was sheriff, he spent several hours a week sharpening his reflexes and his marksmanship. He was unbeaten in the fast draw. His speed and showmanship did much to discourage criminals and outlaws. Bat may have disliked killing and violence, but he was one of the Wild West's most successful men with a gun.

QUESTIONS

1. Sometimes we can prove a generalization is faulty by pointing out a fact that makes the generalization false in at least one instance. If, for example, your sister says that all boys play rough games, you may tell her about a friend's brother whose only sports are bowling and ping pong.

Each of the generalizations listed on the left is faulty. In the column at the right, find the statement that proves the generalization false and write the letter in the appropriate blank.

______ Western lawmen were just violent gunslingers with a badge.

______ In the Old West, outlaws were never arrested without a gun battle.

______ Western lawmen died young.

______ No lawman was as fast with the gun as an outlaw like Billy the Kid.

a. Bat Masterson was unbeaten in the fast draw.

b. Masterson lived to be 70 years old.

c. Masterson was a peace-loving man who preferred using a cane to using a gun.

d. Bat captured Dave Rudabaugh and his gang without firing a shot.

8. Judging the Relevance of Information

When you judge the relevance of information, you try to decide whether specific facts or knowledge will be helpful in solving a problem.

Let's say you are trying to get into a next-door neighbor's garage to rescue the neighbor's dog, and a little boy says he knows where the key to the garage is. This is relevant information. It helps you solve the problem. If, however, the little boy tells you that the dog's name is Rex, this is not particularly helpful in gaining entry to the garage.

If a young student is trying to earn money and the student's uncle says that the local grocery is employing carryout boys and girls, this is relevant information. Even if the student does not get employed by the grocery, the information is directly related to the problem — earning money. Relevant information doesn't automatically solve the problem, but it is clearly related to a possible answer to the difficulty one is facing.

1. Read the situations below and decide whether the information given with each problematic situation is relevant to the solution of the problem. Write ***yes*** if relevant, ***no*** if not relevant.

______a. You are trying to find a safe place to cross a wide river on foot. Your uncle tells you that this particular river is considered to be one of the most beautiful in the country. Is the information your uncle offers *relevant* information?

______b. You are attempting to choose a VCR for an aunt. A friend shows you an ad for some VCR's that are on sale. Is the information the friend offers *relevant*?

______c. Tim Johnson broke his arm at the picnic. His cousin offered to show how he could revive a person who had stopped breathing. Is the information offered by the cousin *relevant* information?

______d. Rosario is making posters for the Fourth of July celebration. Kim Mandarin offers to show Rosario how to write with Chinese characters. Is the information that Kim offers *relevant* information?

______e. Roberto Romano is trying to build a bridge across the creek behind his house. Terry Field offers to show Roberto drawings of hanging bridges and plank bridges that were built by early pioneers in this country. Is the information offered by Terry *relevant* information?

Answers: Did you write "yes" beside b and e? These contain the most relevant information.

A LONELY TRIP TO THE POLE

In 1978 Naomi Uemura, a 37-year-old Japanese adventurer, became the first person in history to travel to the North Pole alone by dog sled. Five different groups of explorers had traveled overland to the North Pole before Uemura. However, none had dared to cross the frozen, wind-swept expanses of ice and snow alone. There had been stories of explorers falling asleep and freezing to death in the frigid darkness. Some scientists even wondered if a person could remain sane under such trying conditions without anyone to see or talk to for weeks at a time.

Uemura began his 800-kilometer (480-mile), 57-day trip from Cape Edward on Ellsmere Island in the Canadian Arctic. It wasn't long before he ran into trouble. One of his sled dogs gave birth, causing a delay. Soon afterwards a hungry polar bear tried to attack Uemura and his dogs. At one time Uemura was trapped on an ice floe about the size of a football field. It had broken away from the rest of the ice. Uemura had to wait for the water between his ice floe and the mainland to freeze before he could continue his journey.

Uemura carried a tiny radio with which he sent a signal to the Smithsonian Institution in Washington, D.C., when he arrived at the North Pole. The signal was relayed from a satellite.

QUESTIONS

1. This selection describes how the trip was difficult.
Which of the following items of information is most relevant to this point?

a. Five different groups of explorers had gone overland to the North Pole.
b. One of his sled dogs gave birth.
c. He sent a signal to the Smithsonian Institution in Washington, D.C.

2. The selection emphasizes how dangerous the trip was. Which of the following items is most relevant to this point?

a. He was alone.
b. He started from Ellsmere Island.
c. His radio signal was relayed by satellite.

LEARNING TO SURVIVE AT SEA

You have probably heard about people who were shipwrecked and found themselves floating helplessly on the open sea. Many of these people died from thirst, starvation, or exposure to the sun.

A French doctor, Alain Bombard, believed that people who were shipwrecked could survive if they learned to protect and feed themselves. He believed that a person adrift in an open boat could drink sea water a little at a time. He also believed that the tiny, drifting aquatic creatures in the water, called plankton, could be used as food. On October 19, 1953, he set out from France by himself on a voyage to prove his theory.

Dr. Bombard was careful to drink no more than 0.7 liters (1 1/2 pints) of sea water every day. For food, he pulled a closely woven net behind the boat to catch the plankton floating near the surface of the water. He also caught fish with a small harpoon. He was often able to squeeze fresh drinking water from the fish he caught.

Dr. Bombard's voyage was very challenging. He became weak from his poor diet, and he developed a painful rash. He thought of giving up his experiment but decided to continue.

He reached the West Indies on Christmas Eve. He was exhausted and thin, but he had proved that people can survive at sea without taking supplies of food or fresh water with them. He had survived a 2,820 mile voyage.

QUESTIONS

1. Which information is most relevant to what Dr. Bombard was trying to prove?

   a. He set out from France.
   b. He ended his trip on Christmas Eve.
   c. He survived a 2,820-mile voyage.

2. Which information is most relevant in explaining why he was able to do what he did?

   a. Many shipwrecked people die of exposure to the sun.
   b. He drank 0.7 liters of sea water every day.
   c. He developed a rash.

USING LIGHT FOR CONVERSATIONS

Telephone cables have been immensely improved by the use of thin threads of ultrapure glass, the thickness of a human hair, which transmit beams of laser light. This system, called fiber optics, is used to carry voice, data, and video signals.

Light signals in optical fibers can send much more information than electrical signals in copper cables can. A bundle of twenty fibers, no thicker than a pencil, can handle 76,200 telephone calls daily. A copper cable three inches in diameter, containing 1,800 separate wires, can handle only 900 conversations! Optical fibers weigh only one percent as much as copper cables. They occupy less space. Signals in copper wires need to be made stronger by special boosters every 300 to 600 feet. The same signals can run for many miles in optical fiber without having to be reamplified.

Fiber optics systems have been tested in Chicago by AT&T and in Santa Monica, California, by California Bell Telephone. Copper cables are currently being replaced by fiber bundles in the United States. Eventually the whole country will be served by these new fiber bundles.

The advent of fiber optics heralds an era of greatly increased telephone use. In the future, thanks partly to the efficiency of the new technology, people will use the telephone to call libraries, newspapers, and magazines with the idea of automatically receiving information about news events, travel, sports, fashions, and other subjects. The telephone may be used for voting in elections, for making purchases from department stores, and for playing games coast to coast using video monitors.

QUESTIONS

1. Which information is most relevant to explaining the advantage of fiber optics?

a. They are only the thickness of a human hair.
b. They carry signals.
c. They have been tested in Chicago.

2. What item of information do you think is most relevant to the telephone companies' decision to begin using fiber optics?

a. The fibers are made of glass.
b. They carry more information than copper cables.
c. Telephones can be used for making purchases from department stores.

ELECTRIC CARS AGAIN

In the year 1834, fifty years before the production of "modern" gasoline-powered automobiles, Thomas Davenport, an American blacksmith, built a working electric car. In 1899 an electric car was the first car to reach a speed of 60 miles per hour.

Electric cars continued to be improved, and by 1900, 38 percent of all cars were electric. Twenty companies were building these vehicles. The electric car of the early 1900's was maneuverable and durable, required little maintenance, and was instant-start, vibration free, safe, and economical. With all of these favorable points, it still did not remain on the market. The batteries were too bulky and too weak. It could travel only about 100 miles before the batteries needed recharging. The combustion engine was more efficient, and gasoline was cheap.

By the 1970's gasoline had become expensive, and batteries were enormously improved. A tiny power cell could run a wristwatch for a year. Nevertheless, the battery in cars was still the relatively inefficient lead-acid type invented in 1860.

During this period, the Argonne National Laboratory began experimenting with new battery types, and by the early 1980's scientists had produced a lithium-metal-sulfide battery that produces 70 to 100 watt-hours per kilogram (about 2 1/5 pounds). It lasts 300 to 1,000 cycles (a cycle is a charge and a discharge). In comparison, golf cart batteries deliver only 25 to 35 watt hours per kilogram and last 200 to 300 cycles. To sum up, the new batteries last longer and are three times more powerful.

Soon the new batteries may be further refined so that they can be used for electric passenger cars. One obstacle yet remaining for these lithium-metal-sulfide batteries is their excessively high cost. Methods must be found to reduce this cost before their use is practical for large-scale use in cars.

QUESTIONS

1. Which item of information is most relevant when considering the disadvantage of electric cars?

   a. Their durability and safety.
   b. The amount of maintenance they require.
   c. The cost of batteries.

2. The selection makes the point that electric cars were popular in 1900. Which item of information is most relevant to this point?

   a. Thomas Davenport built a working electric car in 1834.
   b. Twenty companies were building these cars.
   c. Car batteries are of the lead-acid type invented in 1860.

3. The author of this story tells us that the new lithium-metal-sulfide type of battery is an improvement. What relevant information supports this conclusion?

   a. It was developed by Argonne National Laboratory.
   b. By 1900, 38 percent of all cars were electric.
   c. The new battery produces 70 to 100 watt-hours per kilogram.

KIRLIAN PHOTOGRAPHY

Semyon Kirlian, discoverer of the Kirlian Effect, was a largely self-educated electrician living in the Russian city of Krasnodar. In 1939, using equipment at a local hospital, he took photographs of his own hand. When the photographic plate was developed, a mysterious glow appeared around the finger tips. He next took pictures of a fresh-cut leaf and saw that it was also surrounded by a glow. Its surface was spangled by tiny pinpoints of light. If a piece of a leaf was cut off, the photograph still showed the outline of the entire leaf, but the cut off section was dimmer. A coin showed a faint glow but no points of light.

Psychologist Dr. Thelma Moss of the University of California's center for Health Sciences became interested in this phenomenon in the early 1970's. Moss went to the Soviet Union to confer with researchers there. Back in California in 1971, she and one of her students set about developing duplicates of some of the devices Russian scientists had been using in Kirlian research.

Other investigators, such as Dr. Stanley Krippner and William Tiller of Stanford University's Department of Materials Science, followed Moss's lead. By May 1972 Kirlian research was advanced enough to call a Western Hemisphere Conference on Kirlian Photography.

Research continues, though there are many skeptics who distrust the research and the supposed findings. Moss has reported 100-percent success in using Kirlian Photography to predict the ability of soybean seeds to germinate. She has also made videotapes showing plant auras getting brighter at the approach of a human hand.

QUESTIONS

1. What relevant information do you need to answer the who-what-when-where questions below? Match the letter of the right answer to each of the questions.

______Who?	a. 1939
______What?	b. Semyon Kirlian
______When?	c. Krasnodar, Russia
______Where?	d. An odd glow surrounding figures in a photograph.

2. Based on the information in the story, you might conclude that Kirlian research has the potential to be directly useful in an economic sense. Which information is most relevant to this conclusion?

a. Semyon Kirlian was a largely self-educated electrician.
b. Dr. Thelma Moss went to the Soviet Union to confer with researchers.
c. Dr. Moss claims she can, using Kirlian Photography, predict the ability of soybean seeds to germinate.

3. Which information is most relevant in explaining what Kirlian Photography is supposedly all about?

a. Kirlian used equipment in a local hospital.
b. In Kirlian's photographs of his own hand, a mysterious glow appeared around the finger tips.
c. In 1972 a Western Hemisphere Conference on Kirlian Photography was held.

ANIMAL OR PLANT

In past centuries people could not tell whether a sponge was a plant or an animal. About 150 years ago a scientist studied sponges under a microscope. He found that water went in some openings and came out others. The water contained tiny plants and animals when it was taken in, but it did not have them when it was discarded. The scientist concluded that the sponge was an animal which had "eaten" the tiny plants and animals.

Sponges are the most primitive of the many-celled animals. They eat, grow, and reproduce but do not have sense organs, nerves, tentacles, or leglike parts. Adult sponges cannot move from place to place.

How does this curious animal function? Outer layers of a sponge consist of flat cells. Inside there are long canals with very unusual cells which function like filters. Tiny, whiplike threads, or lashers, beat the water, forcing out tiny plants and animals. The lashers also serve to force food and oxygen into the cells.

Most sponges grow in the sea, though a few are adapted to fresh water. They attach themselves to a rock or the sea bottom. Their shape may be irregular or may resemble a glass, ball, glove, cup, or cane. Their size may be as small as a pinhead or as large as six feet around. Large sponges can weigh up to 90 pounds. Colors include red, orange, brown, green, yellow, and white.

Some sponge skeletons are made of spicules, needlelike forms of calcium or silicon. Others have spongin fibers, which are a protein material resembling silk in chemical makeup. When sponges are prepared for market, the soft, living cells are cleansed out so that only the spicule or spongin skeleton is sold. These skeletons absorb liquid easily and in large amounts.

QUESTIONS

1. The selection tells us that sponges are primitive many-celled animals. Which statement below is most relevant to this point?

   a. They eat, grow, and reproduce.
   b. Large sponges weigh up to 90 pounds.
   c. The spongin fibers of sponges absorb water easily and in large amounts.

2. What information below is most relevant to the discovery that sponges are animals?

   a. Water going into a sponge was seen to contain tiny plants and animals, but not when it came out.
   b. Sponges may resemble a glass, ball, glove, cup, or cane.
   c. Spicules are needlelike forms of calcium or silicon.

3. The selection describes how sponges function as animals. Which information is most relevant to this?

   a. What lashers do.
   b. The shape, size, and color of sponges.
   c. How sponges are prepared for market.

9. Analyzing Persuasive Techniques

We are bombarded by millions of words every day. Many of these words appear in cleverly phrased messages and advertisements. Billboards, newspapers, magazines, TV, and radio programs as well as clerks and salespeople try hard to persuade us to buy special products and services. Advertising has become a fine art and a multibillion dollar business.

The writers who think up advertising slogans and catchy phrases know how to appeal to our most basic interests and concerns. Here are some of the typical strategies they use:

a. They realize that we like to feel important. So they tell us that their products will make us glamorous and sophisticated.

b. They know that we want to feel confident and proud of our purchases. So they inform us that their products are well made, carefully tested, and reliable.

c. The ad writers know that we want to get the most for our money. So they offer us spectacular savings, magnificent bargains, and super sales.

d. The people who dream up the ads have discovered that we are a bit lazy. They quickly assure us that their products are foolproof and easy-to-use.

e. Fear of failure is something that haunts each of us. Some advertisers suggest that their learning machines and instructional materials will help children avoid the pitfalls of disappointment.

f. Some of the more clever advertisers have figured out that we like to think of ourselves as kindly and considerate. So they urge us to send a card or a gift (usually an expensive one) that will show that we truly care.

We can abbreviate these advertising techniques by labeling them as follows:

Glamorous You	***Great Savings***	***Avoiding Failure***
Top Quality	***Easy- to-Use***	***Showing You Care***

1. Read each of the statements below and decide which technique is being used. Write one of the six labels from the list above in the blank beside each ad.

______________________ a. Show your friends that you remember them during those special times in the year. Send a bountiful bouquet!

______________________ b. Join the "In" crowd. Our new fall styles will make you more attractive than ever!

______________________ c. Even a child can assemble our gadgets. Just follow the simple directions.

________ d. Don't let the kids on the block outshine your children. Our modern references are keyed for academic success.

________ e. We are practically giving away the store. We have cut prices to the bone.

________ f. Our prices are unbelievable! There are closeouts in every department.

________ g. Go to the top of the class! Our success-oriented learning materials help build essential skills.

________ h. When you use our kitchen appliances, cleaning up is fast — and almost fun!

________ i. When you splash on our perfume, heads will turn. You'll discover a new world.

________ j. Our tires cost a little more, but when you buy them you tell your children that their safety really counts.

________ k. Don't buy new shoes until you have checked our prices. We will not be undersold!

________ l. Sign up for our first-aid course today. When accidents occur, you'll know what to do.

________ m. Our 4-wheel Renegades have won tough terrain road races all over the world. American roads are no challenge for Renegades!

________ n. Tough laboratory tests have confirmed the long-lasting durability of our washers.

________ o. There can be a new you. Our jewelry adds sparkle to your evening wear and highlights your natural beauty.

Answers:

a. Showing You Care
b. Glamorous You
c. Easy-to-Use
d. Avoiding Failure
e. Great Savings
f. Great Savings
g. Avoiding Failure
h. Easy-to-Use
i. Glamorous You
j. Showing You Care
k. Great Savings
l. Avoiding Failure
m. Top Quality
n. Top Quality
o. Glamorous You

A LETTER FROM *CITIZENS TO HELP THE POOR*

Tonight in this city, several thousand people will go to bed hungry. Some don't even have homes; they sleep in the streets. Most of these people do not have warm clothing or decent shoes. They are our city's poor.

Won't you let these people know you are concerned about them? Our group will show you the way to help. With our shelters for the homeless, we provide the best care for the poor. And we provide that care at an incredibly low cost to you. Only 17 cents a day can protect the life of a man, woman, or child. All contributions are tax deductible, and our monthly payment plan makes your charitable contribution simple to manage.

So won't you help? Call one of our shelters today for more information. Don't disappoint these hungry, cold people. Don't disappoint yourself.

QUESTIONS

1. "Won't you let these people know you are concerned about them?" is an example of which persuasive technique?

a. Showing You Care.
b. Top Quality.
c. Glamorous You.

2. Which statement below is an example of the technique "Easy-to-Use"?

a. Our group will show you the way.
b. Only 17 cents a day can protect the life of a man, woman, or child.
c. Our monthly payment plan makes your charitable contribution simple to manage.

3. Which persuasive technique is *least* likely to appear in an advertisement for a charity?

a. Showing You Care.
b. Top Quality.
c. Glamorous You.

4. The technique "Top Quality" is used in which of the statements below?

a. Will you let these people know you are concerned about them?
b. We provide the best care for the poor.
c. Don't disappoint these people.

IF I'M ELECTED...

It was campaign time in Booneville High School, and Juanita and Antonio were running against each other for student council president. On the day before the election, Juanita and Antonio made speeches to the student body in an assembly. After a short introduction, Juanita spoke first:

"Are you tired of a student council president who ignores the students? Are you tired of a student council president who is a poor leader? Are you tired of a student council president who plans dances and then backs out at the last minute? If so, then vote for me. I won't ignore you, and I'll follow through with plans and promises. With my experience as student council secretary, I'm the best person for the job. Let the council know that you care about your school. Don't take chances. Win with Juanita!"

Once Juanita finished, Antonio began his speech:

"I want to be student council president because I can do a good job. I know what I'm doing. The students who know me know that I will work hard for the school and for each of you. I've been a basketball player, an office helper, and an honor student, so I think I have lots of knowledge about our school and about the way to get things done. If you want a strong leader for student council president, vote for me. And remember — Go with Antonio!"

QUESTIONS

Glamorous You	*Great Savings*	*Avoiding Failure*
Top Quality	*Easy-to-Use*	*Showing You Care*

1. Read each of the statements from Juanita's speech below and decide which techniques she is using. Select your answers from the box above and write them in the blanks next to the statement.

   ____________ a. "With my experience as student council secretary, I'm the best person for the job."

   ____________ b. "Let the council know you care about your school."

   ____________ c. "Don't take chances. Win with Juanita!"

2. Which of the following persuasive techniques do you feel Antonio stresses most in his speech?

   a. Glamorous You
   b. Easy-to-Use
   c. Top Quality
   d. Avoiding Failure
   e. Great Savings
   f. Showing You Care

3. If one of the candidates had said she or he could provide school activities for less cost to the school and students, which persuasive technique would this candidate be using?

a. Avoiding Failure
b. Top Quality
c. Great Savings

4. Let's assume that the candidate who uses the largest number of persuasive techniques will win the election. Based on this assumption, who will be Booneville High School's next student council president?

a. Juanita
b. Antonio

A WORD FROM OUR SPONSOR...

One rainy Sunday afternoon a girl named Bonita and her sister Kelly sat down to watch an old movie on television. The girls had been looking forward to the movie all week. But after an hour passed they soon realized that they were seeing more commercials than the movie itself.

First came a commercial with a famous tennis player. He was trying to get people to buy Sprints tennis shoes. "If I don't wear my Sprints," he said, "I'll never reach those tough shots." He jumped up and down a few times, then ran across the screen. "Don't *you* be left behind in that big game—buy Sprints today!" The tennis player's smile faded from the screen.

The next commercial began with a conversation between two women on the beach. "Lynn, that new bathing suit you're wearing is gorgeous," the blonde woman said.

Lynn smiled and turned around to show off her suit. "Thanks, Melissa—it's a designer suit, the best there is! It's made of the strongest material—and it fits me perfectly, not like cheaper bathing suits."

Melissa sighed. "It must have cost a bundle."

Lynn laughed. "No, that's the best part. I bought it at Worthing's fantastic summer clearance sale for half of what I paid last year. Hey, Melissa—where are you going?"

"I'm going to Worthing's," Melissa yelled as she ran down the beach. "I want to look like a beauty queen for half the price, too!" The commercial ended with an announcer explaining the dates and times of the sale.

Bonita decided she was tired of commercials. "Come on, Kelly," she said as she switched off the television. "Let's go make some brownies." Kelly shook her head. "We don't know how, Bonita."

"We can figure it out," Bonita said. "It couldn't be simpler with that new brownie mix Mom bought."

Kelly laughed. "Bonita, you sound just like a commercial!"

QUESTIONS

1. Which of the following persuasive techniques does the tennis player use in the commercial for Sprints shoes?

   a. Easy-to-Use
   b. Showing You Care
   c. Avoiding Failure

2. Choose the statement below that contains the same persuasive technique as the Sprints advertisement.

   a. Invest in gold now — never before have you been able to buy so much for so little.
   b. Use V'room motor oil, and your car will always be a winner.
   c. Slickstick lipstick can put some dazzle into your life.

3. Which of the following statements would be in the Sprints commercial if the advertisers wanted to use the "Showing You Care" technique?

   a. Sprints are the fastest shoes on the market.
   b. Let your little leaguer know you are concerned about his game. Buy Sprints.
   c. Buy Sprints, the sneakers that look good and feel good.

4. There are several persuasive techniques in the bathing suit commercial. Match the letter of the persuasive technique on the right with the advertising statement on the left.

______ "It's a designer suit, the best there is!"	a. Glamorous You
______ "I want to look like a beauty queen."	b. Great Savings
______ "I bought it at Worthing's fantastic clearance sale for half of what I paid last year."	c. Top Quality

5. Which of the following advertising techniques does Bonita use to persuade Kelly to make brownies?

   a. Top Quality
   b. Great Savings
   c. Easy-to-Use

10. Author Bias

Authors are like all other human beings. They have feelings and opinions, and they frequently emphasize these in their writings. It is natural to try to persuade others to accept your point of view. We call this *author bias*.

A person with a bias has definite feelings for or against something. For example, a particular author may feel strongly about protecting nature. He or she may write articles urging us to build more wild-life preserves, save endangered animals, control pollution, and regulate hunting and fishing activities. This author may be constantly gathering evidence regarding problems in the environment. When we read an article by such a writer, we are likely to find that he or she will: (a) choose words to influence or reinforce certain attitudes about conservation on the part of the reader; (b) play upon our sympathies by citing individual instances in which violations of the environment are apparent; and (c) emphasize the point that both our accepted traditions and our cherished heroes have supported the cause being championed. The truly biased author may even leave out important information if it weakens or detracts from the argument being presented.

Using Words to Influence Others

The words writers use give us interesting clues to their thoughts and biases. A soldier who is very cautious may be described by one author as "careful" and "prudent." He is commended for his natural healthy concern in protecting his own life. He isn't foolish. He doesn't take unnecessary chances. The same soldier may be portrayed by another writer as cowardly and spineless. The second writer tells us that the soldier's obsession with his own safety puts others at risk and does nothing to support the cause of his country. The soldier is viewed in a distinctly negative light.

See if you can identify the *most negative* or *most uncomplimentary* description in each of the sets of sentences below.

1. a. John was calm at the scene of the accident.
b. John was an observer at the scene of the accident.
c. John was indifferent at the scene of the accident.

2. a. Terry is a strong leader.
b. Terry is a domineering type of person.
c. Terry is an energetic leader.

3. a. Joe Thompson was an unemployed refugee.
b. Joe Thompson was a jobless person.
c. Joe Thompson was an idle outcast.

4. a. We had never seen anything like it. It was absurd.
b. We had never seen anything like it. It was unusual.
c. We had never seen anything like it. It was fantastic.

Answers: Did you select c in the first set, b in the second, c in the third set, and a in the fourth set? These are the correct answers.

Citing Individual Cases

Citing individual cases is an excellent way of capturing reader sympathy. Joseph Stalin, the Russian dictator, once remarked that the death of an individual is a tragedy, but the deaths of thousands is a statistic. We can normally summon up much more sympathy for an individual we know personally than for hundreds or thousands of people we have never met.

5. Pick out the two situations below in which the personal lives and circumstances of individuals or their families are emphasized.

a. The farmers of America have had difficult times. They cannot sell their crops for decent prices, and more and more of them are having to find other kinds of work.
b. Tim Johnson rode his tractor for the last time yesterday. He rode it on a lonely trip to the auction barn where it was sold to the highest bidder. Tomorrow Tim's home and barn will be sold as well.
c. It has been a costly flood. Millions of acres of land are now under water, and residents of the valley have had to seek higher ground.
d. The airline has not released the names of the crash victims, but it is expected that losses will be high. The FAA is investigating the causes of the tragedy.
e. Little Sally Roberts stood beside a huge pile of her family's belongings in the middle of Chicago Avenue. Her parents were frantically seeking a place to stay before the night closed in upon them.

Answers: Did you put a check beside B and E? These are the correct answers.

Citing Great Traditions and Leaders

It is common to back up arguments by citing great traditions and recognized leaders who support your cause.

6. Pick out the two statements below which use this technique.

a. The right to strike is a cherished privilege of American laborers. We have had this right for over a century. It is time for us to use this great weapon in our search for decent treatment.
b. We have lost our jobs, our homes, and our futures.
c. Each community should care for its own citizens. This is the American Way.

Answers: a and c.

WOLVES

Read the two selections describing wolves below and answer the questions.

Selection 1

Wolves are the lions of North America. Like lions, they live in family groups and work together to catch their prey. Like lions, wolves are majestic animals. In fact, some of them even have ruffs of hair that look very much like the manes of lions.

When we consider all of these striking similarities, it is strange that many people admire lions but dislike wolves. Lions are called "lordly" and "noble"; wolves are often described as "cruel" and "sneaky."

"Man's best friend," the dog, is really a descendant of wolves that were domesticated in the Middle East about 12,000 years ago. Most of the traits that people admire in dogs — their loyalty, their intelligence, their friendliness — have come from wolves.

Selection 2

Wolves have always been the enemies of sheep herders and cattle ranchers. When they are on the prowl, these ugly killers of the forest can terrorize huge herds. Frantic cows and ewes have little or no chance of protecting their young. The snarling wolves attack in large groups. They snatch frightened calves and lambs on every side. These treacherous, bloodthirsty beasts often mangle their innocent prey simply to satisfy their cruel need for power. They frequently leave the mutilated carcasses of their victims without eating any of the meat.

Wolves are even cruel to each other on occasion. The leader of the pack is usually the largest and strongest. He lords it over the others. He snarls and snaps at other members of the group if they do not obey him. In turn, the stronger wolves under him force weaker wolves to do their bidding. The lives of the lowest-ranking members of the pack are often filled with fear and anxiety. The cruel law of the jungle seems to be the only code of living these fierce creatures know.

Tim Perry had a sheep ranch near the Canadian border for 20 years, but the wolves have finally ruined his herds. He is giving up and moving to Vermont. Tim claims that he had every right to protect his herds with poisoned meat, but the authorities were not willing to let him use the poison to save his animals. Tim believes that the cherished right to protect his property, a right guaranteed by our Constitution and our traditions, has been violated.

QUESTIONS

It is obvious that these two accounts present very different views of wolves. Both authors describe facts that support their own personal points of view and ignore other facts. In addition, both use positive and negative words. The second author also cites an individual case as well as tradition to make the point.

1. Notice the positive words in the first paragraph in the first story — *fascinating, family groups, majestic.* What three words in the last paragraph of the same story help develop a positive attitude toward wolves?

   a. ____________________
   b. ____________________
   c. ____________________

2. In the second story, the author cites an individual case to gain your sympathies. What is this individual case?

   ____

   ____

3. In this same story the author refers to a great tradition to support his argument. What is the tradition he cites?

   ____

   ____

AN UNREALIZED DREAM

About 2,000 years ago people began to think about turning one substance into another. The great ancient Greek philosopher Aristotle had said that all substances are made of the same four "elements." The only difference from substance to substance is in the proportions of the four elements. Aristotle's views were popular in the classical world and all through the Middle Ages. Influenced partly by the beliefs of this great theoretician, people began to wonder: Why can't you change something common in nature, such as a rock or water, into something rare, such as gold? Some people set about to do just that. They used a kind of primitive science along with magic in their searches. These early experimenters are known today as *alchemists*. The idea that excited a great many alchemists was the belief that lead could be turned into gold. The alchemists tried all sorts of experiments with lead, heating it, mixing it with other substances, and so on.

Frustrated by their failures, some alchemists turned to the idea that maybe somewhere in the world there is a magic stone, the *philosopher's stone,* which would do the job for them of turning lead or other metals into gold. With their usual energy they searched far and wide but never found the marvelous substance.

To keep all of their findings secret, each alchemist developed a code of odd symbols. These marvelously clever codes soon became so complicated that one alchemist could not read another's writings.

The work of the alchemists was frequently supported by princes. The trouble for the alchemists was that when they failed in the quest for gold, they were likely to be sent into exile or executed.

And fail they did, of course. As reasonable as their pursuits seemed, they were doomed to failure. But despite this, alchemy produced many distinguished thinkers who helped to found the modern science of chemistry.

One of these was the Englishman Roger Bacon, who lived in the 1200's. Bacon had a deep belief in the direct observation of nature. He was learned in mathematics and astronomy. But he was also an alchemist, and his often brilliant writings combine his beliefs derived from alchemy with his scientific observations.

In the 1500's another great alchemist, the Swiss thinker Paracelsus, combined alchemy with suggestions for new approaches to medicine. In particular, he promoted the use of specific remedies for diseases, an idea of considerable importance in later developments in medicine.

Belief in alchemy finally began to die out in the 1600's. By then researchers were turning to more rigorous approaches toward chemical observations. This culminated in the 1700's with the experiments of the Frenchman Lavoisier, the founder of modern chemistry. Alchemy was dead without ever having produced a single bar of gold.

QUESTIONS

1. The author of this article is in general –

a. Sympathetic toward the alchemists.
b. Unsympathetic toward the alchemists.

2. The author describes Aristotle as "the great theoretician." This helps to make the searches of the alchemists seem –

a. Reasonable, even though futile.
b. Ridiculous.

3. In paragraph 1, the author says the alchemists used a kind of primitive "science" and calls them "early experimenters." What other descriptive words might the author have used in place of these to give a different tone to the selection?

a. "Science": ____________________
b. "Early experimenters": ____________________

4. The author says that "the alchemists tried all sorts of experiments with lead, heating it, mixing it with other substances, and so on." Which word in this statement is particularly helpful in expressing the author's biases?

____

5. The last sentence in paragraph 2 also contains some loaded words. What are they?

____

6. To support the selection's biases the author cites the individual accomplishments of —

a. Bacon
b. Lavoisier

7. Paracelsus is presented in a favorable light. What descriptive words or phrases in the first sentence of paragraph 7 help to accomplish this? (Select two or more words and phrases.)

____

____

A LIMITED MIRACLE

In 1939 Paul Muller, a Swiss research chemist, was testing chemicals that might be used to eliminate insect pests. The one he found most effective was DDT, a chemical first discovered by a German scientist in 1874. In 1941 DDT wiped out Colorado potato beetles on Swiss farms. In 1948 Muller was awarded the Nobel prize for his discovery.

During World War II DDT was used widely, particularly by Americans. It proved effective in destroying the cotton pest, the boll weevil, as well as other agricultural pests, and this dramatically increased agricultural yields. It controlled malaria, yellow fever, and other diseases carried by insects. In fact, it brought about a revolution in public health.

There were problems, though. Insects are able to build up an immunity to DDT. Furthermore, DDT kills not only harmful insects, but also the insects that eat the pests. When these pest-eating insects are not around any more, the pests multiply much more rapidly.

The worst problem with DDT is that it has a residual effect. Such organisms as fish and crabs build up the poison in their systems. By the 1960's there were reports of DDT accumulation in the forests of Maine. Penguins and seals in the Antarctic showed significant buildups of DDT.

The most severe effects were those on birds. Peregrine falcons received so much DDT through their food that by the mid 1960's they were no longer producing young. The osprey, as a result of contamination, produced soft-shelled eggs which broke in the nest. DDT had begun to become a tremendous threat to the natural environment.

Finally, in 1972, the Environmental Protection Agency banned the use of DDT except by special permit. Since 1972 DDT accumulations in the environment have slowly decreased, and there has been gradual improvement of conditions in swamps, oceans, lakes, forests, and prairies. The miracle, in the end, turned out to be a widespread killer.

QUESTIONS

1. In this article, the author gives –

a. Only the positive aspects of DDT use.
b. Only the negative aspects of DDT use.
c. Both the positive and the negative aspects of DDT use.

2. What is the author's opinion about DDT?

a. She thinks the chemical is more harmful than helpful.
b. She believes DDT should be used with no restriction.
c. She feels DDT is not as harmful as most people think.

3. What accepted tradition is supported by the author's opinion of DDT?

a. Nature should not be tampered with.
b. People should have the freedom to change their environment.
c. Technological progress is more important than the protection of endangered species.

4. The author begins the story by describing the benefits of DDT. In what paragraph does she first describe the drawbacks of using the chemical?

a. Paragraph 3
b. Paragraph 4
c. Paragraph 5

5. Based on her conclusions about DDT, which of the following items seems of the greatest value to the author?

a. Insect control.
b. The Nobel Prize.
c. Wildlife safety.

The author cites several individual cases to show both the benefits and the drawbacks of using DDT. In each of the pairs of sentences below, place a ***P*** before the positive use of the chemical and an ***N*** before the negative use of DDT.

6. ____________ Improved living conditions for soldiers.
____________ The osprey's soft-shelled eggs.

7. ____________ Build-ups of DDT in Antarctic penguins.
____________ A revolution in public health.

8. ____________ DDT accumulation in Maine forests.
____________ Destruction of agricultural pests.

D. Putting It All Together

The second section of this book contains ten stories, with several questions after each story. The questions test you on your ability to handle all the skills taught in this book. Next to each one is a box that lists the skills you need to answer the question. If you wish, you can go back to the chapter in which the skill was taught for a quick review.

1. Underwater Discoveries

For centuries the people of Takashima, on the island of Kyushu, Japan, have been finding strange objects in their underwater fishing nets. All of these relics are from the 13th century, from two great naval battles between Japanese defending their homeland and huge forces of Mongol invaders from across the sea in China.

The Mongols, under their great emperor Kublai Khan, had conquered all of China. The Khan's armies had extended his empire from Persia in the west to Korea in the east. Japan was his next goal. He decided to build a navy that would cover the sea.

Late in 1274 Kublai mounted his first attack. He had 900 ships plus 25,000 men and their horses, as well as 15,000 Korean troops. The armada weighed anchor off the shore of Kyushu and attacked at dawn. The Japanese counterattacked, and there was fierce fighting. The Mongols were winning, when a huge cloud appeared. It was a typhoon. The Mongols hurried to their ships to protect them and rode out the storm on the open sea. Afterward they limped back to China with a loss of more than 13,000 men.

In 1281 the Khan's second invasion got underway with a total of 4,500 ships, 50,000 of the Khan's soldiers, and 20,000 Koreans. Two thousand five hundred of the ships then picked up 100,000 more soldiers in South China. The huge fleet sailed to the island of Iki off Japan and captured it. The ships next sailed toward Kyushu. When they neared the shore, they opened fire. Arrows sped through the air. Artillery hurled rocks and pots of naphtha. Drums beat and horns blasted to scare the Japanese horses.

The Mongols could not advance because the Japanese army stood firm. Then the Japanese navy attacked from the open sea and set the Mongol ships on fire. The battle continued for six weeks. Once again, a typhoon blew in. This time the typhoon sank a huge number of the Mongol ships and thwarted the invasion. The Japanese called the typhoon a "divine wind" because they felt they had been protected by mysterious, unseen forces.

The Mongols' threat to Japan was finally finished. Kublai Khan wanted to organize a third expedition, but his advisers were against it. The objects that occasionally show up in the nets of Takashima fisherman are reminders of the incredible defeats that Kublai Khan and his armies suffered.

QUESTIONS

FIGURATIVE LANGUAGE

1. "He decided to build a navy that would cover the sea."
   This sentence contains an example of –

   a. Hyperbole.
   b. Personification.
   c. Simile.

CAUSE-EFFECT

2. The Mongol defeat in the second invasion was the result of several causes. What were these causes?

____

____

____

PROBLEMS WITH GENERALIZATIONS

3. "All of these relics are from the 13th century." What word in the sentence above is probably too restrictive?

____

2. Trembling Hands That See

The Navaho Indians practice one of the most mysterious forms of divination known anywhere. The American anthropologist Dr. Clyde Kluckhohn studied their methods and reported on his experiences, especially those he had with the Navaho diviner Gregorio.

While on the Navaho reservation on a field trip, Mrs. Kluckhohn lost her handbag. The Kluckhohns told Gregorio what had happened. The diviner rolled up his sleeves, carefully washed his arms and hands, and climbed slowly to the top of a hill. While facing north, he sprinkled corn pollen on his right hand and the hand began to tremble. Next he rubbed the palms of his hands together, and a short time later his left hand began to tremble, too. Gregorio repeated this ritual several times with his eyes closed. He then slowly moved both hands as if to form the outlines of a bag. Finally, he informed the Kluckhohns that the bag could be found at the local trading post. It was just as Gregorio had predicted.

Diviners like Gregorio regard the trembling of their hands as something beyond their power. This form of divination is almost always used for practical purposes, for example, for locating stray horses and sheep or personal possessions. The hand trembler's art is also used to help treat illness and to help detect underground water.

QUESTIONS

AUTHOR BIAS

1. What kind of opinion does the author have of hand trembling?

a. Favorable.
b. Opposed.
c. Skeptical.

AUTHOR BIAS

2. To support this viewpoint the author uses a number of devices. For example:

a. The reference to Dr. Kluckhohn helps to back up the viewpoint by (in your words) –

____

____

b. The author cites an individual case to back this viewpoint. Which individual case? (Explain in a few words.)

____

____

DETECTING ASSUMPTIONS

3. In the last paragraph the author states that "hand trembling is used for practical purposes." This appears to imply that the author assumes that –

a. Hand trembling works.
b. Hand trembling's effects are uncertain.
c. Hand trembling is poorly understood.

CRITERIA FOR JUDGMENTS

4. Which of the following criteria is most important in evaluating the hand trembler's feats?

a. How much their hands tremble.
b. The percentage of times they are successful.
c. The strength of their beliefs.

PROBLEMS WITH WORDS

5. "The hand trembler's art is also used to help treat illness."
In this sentence the word "art" is used to mean –

a. Deception.
b. Special skill.
c. Thing of beauty.

3. Unsung Heroes

When we read fascinating stories of animals in their natural settings and see gorgeous colored pictures of the animals, few of us realize what some people went through to make all this possible.

Sometimes, just getting to the place where observations of the animals begins can be difficult and dangerous. In Rwanda, Africa, Dian Fossey often had to scramble for hours up 45-degree slopes, jog along muddy paths, hack each step through dense bushes or forests, or crawl through harsh nettles just to reach the gorillas she was studying. In the Philippines, Robert Kennedy had to climb high into a lauan tree to study a rare Philippine eagle. Then he and Ned Rettig crossed a rope to another great tree where a nest held a baby eagle. The 20- foot rope was, of course, difficult to cross, but there was also a wasps' nest in the eagle's tree. When Rettig accidentally bumped a branch near the wasps' nest, the wasps went for Kennedy. At 1,300 feet in the air, he found himself on a rope, being stung repeatedly from head to toe by wasps. But he had to keep his balance or be killed!

To study bats, investigators have to enter caves which can present many problems, including the guano bird droppings, which produce unpleasant ammonia fumes. One cave in Texas, where Merlin Tuttle went to photograph bats, had 20 million of the creatures and tons of guano. Tuttle could breathe only with a respirator. That was not easy with the temperature at 102 degrees and the humidity at 100 percent. His respirator failed little by little, but he didn't notice it.

Eventually, he landed in the hospital with 40 percent of his lung capacity destroyed. Contrary to doctors' predictions he managed to recover. On his first trip after his recovery, he grabbed a tree branch to swing over an abandoned mine shaft. The tree limb broke, and he fell onto large rocks. This time he had broken ribs, cuts, and bruises, but he's ready to go again!

QUESTIONS

CLASSIFICATION

1. How does the author classify the incidents described in this selection?

   a. Beautiful.
   b. Dangerous.
   c. Rewarding.

AUTHOR BIAS

2. The stories of Kennedy and Tuttle are meant by the author to show that –

   a. Nature writers and photographers are very brave.
   b. The animals they study are fascinating.
   c. The stories they write are wonderful.

CAUSE-EFFECT

3. One of the causes of Tuttle's problems in the cave was the fumes from the guano. Another was that his repirator failed.
What were some other causes?

____

____

PROBLEMS WITH WORDS

4. "Fossey had to *scramble* for hours up 45-degree slopes."
In which sentence below does the word "scramble" have a similar meaning to the usage above?

a. I ask my mother to scramble my eggs in the morning.
b. Mice will scramble into any hole to get away from our cat.
c. The word puzzle scrambles letters of words so they are hard to read.

4. A Unique Muscle

Did you know that your tongue is the only muscle in your body which is attached at only one end? It is an extremely important muscle because it helps you chew, taste, and swallow food. It also helps you talk clearly.

The surface of your tongue has about 3,000 taste buds! These are contained in *papillae* (the little "bumps" on your tongue). The papillae give you the amazing ability to differentiate among all of the types of taste, such as sweet, sour, salty, or special flavors such as chocolate.

The taste buds send nerve impulses to the brain. The brain makes you aware of the taste of things. Your tongue will not work properly unless it is moist. Saliva is produced to keep your tongue wet and to aid in swallowing your food. When you swallow, your tongue contracts and pushes the food backward on its journey to your stomach.

In addition to being part of the digestive system, the tongue is an organ of speech. By touching or not touching the lips and teeth, it helps to form sounds. People who are "tongue-tied" cannot speak clearly because their tongues cannot move freely.

Tongues such as ours appear only in animals with backbones. Amphibians have long, powerful tongues to catch insects and other food. Some lizards have broad, plump tongues to help in eating. The forked tongues of snakes are sensitive organs of touch.

QUESTIONS

CLASSIFICATION

1. Match.

_____	Forked tongue.	a. Frog
_____	Long, powerful tongue to catch insects.	b. Rabbit
_____	Tongue similar to that of a human being.	c. Rattler

CAUSE-EFFECT

2. Match each statment with a type of cause-effect relationship.

______	Taste buds make you aware of the taste of things.	a. Direct cause
______	Your tongue will not work properly unless it is moist.	b. Indirect cause
______	Your tongue pushes your food back.	c. Necessary pre-condition

PROBLEMS WITH WORDS

3. Circle the word in each sentence that could have at least two very different meanings.

a. The tongue is an organ of speech.
b. The surface of your tongue has about 3,000 taste buds.
c. A snake's tongue has a fork on it.

PROBLEMS WITH GENERALIZATIONS

4. Which of the following is a faulty generalization?

a. People who cannot speak clearly are "tongue-tied."
b. People who are "tongue-tied" cannot speak clearly.

5. A Toothless Spineball

What looks like a soccer ball covered with spines, has a long skinny bill like a bird, lays leathery eggs like a snake, and has a pouch like a kangaroo? The answer is one of the world's strangest creatures, a combination of mammal, bird, and reptile. It lives in eastern Australia and is called a *spiny anteater.* When a scientist tried to classify it in 1884, he had a hard time. It was finally classified with the mammals, since it has fur and gives milk to its young. But it had to be put into a special subclass called *monotremes* ("one opening") because it has only one bodily opening for waste disposal and reproduction, as is true of birds and reptiles.

The spiny anteater is about a foot long and covered with hollow spines, which barely hide a black fur coat. The broad front feet have spadelike nails for digging. Each hind foot has an especially long nail for grooming the hair under the spines. When the long, sticky tongue picks up ants, it also gets dirt, which is swallowed along with the ants. There are no teeth.

The spiny anteater's egg hatches in a pouch, though no one is sure how it gets there. The baby stays in the pouch like a child in a crib for three months, licking milk directly from the mother's skin.

Should you try to capture a spiny anteater, it will begin to dig under its body, pushing the soil out and up until only a patch of spines shows above the soil. If it is among rocks, it rolls up into a ball. No other animal dares to try to kill the spiny anteater, so it is not an endangered species. A few are killed by cars, but the spiny anteater gets its revenge. Its spines are sharp and hard enough to puncture a tire!

QUESTIONS

FIGURATIVE LANGUAGE

1. The last sentence in paragraph 3 contains an example of –

a. Hyperbole.
b. Personification.
c. Simile.

CLASSIFICATION

2. "*Monotremes* have only one bodily opening for waste disposal and reproduction."
What kind of classification is this?

a. Physical characteristics.
b. Similarities of time or place.
c. Behavior.

CAUSE-EFFECT

3. Which of the following sentences shows a cause-effect relationship?

a. Scientists call the spiny anteater a *monotreme*.
b. No other animal uses the spiny anteater for food, so it is not an endangered species.
c. The spiny anteater's egg hatches in her pouch.

PROBLEMS WITH WORDS

4. In the first sentence of paragraph 3, what does "it" refer to?

a. Spiny anteater.
b. Egg.
c. Pouch.

RELEVANT INFORMATION

5. The author maintains that the spiny anteater is one of the world's strangest creatures.
What information from the selection is most relevant to this statement?

a. It is a combination of mammal, bird, and reptile.
b. It lives in eastern Australia.
c. Its body is covered with hollow spines.

PROBLEMS WITH GENERALIZATIONS

6. In South America, there are anteaters that have long digging claws, no teeth, and a long sticky tongue just like a spiny anteater. Why do you think that the spiny anteater is not classed with them?

a. The spiny anteater has a longer nail on its hind foot.
b. The spiny anteater's reproductive system is very different.
c. The spiny anteater can roll up like a ball.

6. Inexpensive Property

Investing in real estate in the 1980's took a large amount of money. But at least one person figured out a way to make it very reasonable.

The Fiske Planetarium in Boulder, Colorado, announced that it was offering 1,000-acre parcels of land for a mere $20. Now that just seems too good to be true, and there was a catch. The property was located at Olympus Mons, a Texas-sized volcano on the planet Mars.

David Aguilar, the planetarium director, came up with the idea in the hope of raising $1,000 to help with planetarium expenses. Instead, at last count, he had raised $15,000 and was still deluged with requests. Some of these inquiries came from as far away as Japan.

The entire package included the land, a map of Mars, a deed, spaceflight insurance, and such things as instructions on how to use a zero-gravity toilet. There was a stipulation in fine print in the deed that the owner must plant a tree on the land within 20 years, or it would revert to Martian ownership.

The idea appealed to people's imagination, and the novelty seemed to many of them to be well worth the $20 cost. Aguilar now has a new fund-raising gimmick, a guide called *Mars on Ten Dollars a Day*.

QUESTIONS

PERSUASIVE TECHNIQUES

1. Match the elements of the Fiske Planetarium offering on the left with the types of persuasive techniques on the right.

______ 1,000 acres for only $20.	a. Great savings.
______ Helps with planetarium's expenses.	b. Top quality.
______ A complete package, including land, map, deed, etc.	c. Showing you care.

AUTHOR BIAS

2. Which word best describes the author's feeling about Aguilar and his scheme?

a. Clever.
b. Dishonest.
c. Flawed.

DETECTING ASSUMPTIONS

3. The selection tells us that Aguilar has now come up with a guide called *Mars on Ten Dollars a Day*.

What assumption did Aguilar make before he wrote this book?

a. He assumed people will soon be going to Mars.
b. He assumed people would need to know how to live on Mars for ten dollars a day.
c. He assumed people would buy another novelty item to help support the planetarium.

PROBLEMS WITH WORDS

4. What does the word "catch" mean as used in paragraph 2?

a. Concealed difficulty.
b. Something caught.
c. To ensnare.

7. Nauscopie

For nearly 20 years the naval garrison of the island of Ile de France (now Mauritius) watched the colony's beacon keeper, M. Bottineau, demonstrate what he called *nauscopie*. He could predict the arrival of ships and the direction from which they would arrive by scanning the horizon with his naked eye. He never used a telescope.

The theory which he developed was this: A vessel approaching land produces a certain effect on the atmosphere. This means that the ship's approach can be discovered at a great distance by a practiced eye.

All of this sounds simple enough, but no one else except Bottineau could come close to his level of success in prediction. He never really explained his method in depth.

At first Bottineau merely used his special skill to bet sums of money with people at the base regarding the approach of ships. Because of his unusual success, he soon had trouble finding anyone to bet with him.

Between 1778 and 1782 Bottineau correctly forecast the arrival of 575 ships to the island, some of his predictions being made as much as four days in advance. Occasionally a predicted arrival would fail to materialize, but it would usually be found that at the last moment the ship had changed course.

On May 15, 1782, the Minister of Marine in France instructed the governor of Ile de France to record Bottineau's predictions for two years. Bottineau continued to predict the arrival of ships with unerring success. At the end of the experiment he was offered a lump sum of 10,000 livres and a pension of 1,200 livres a year for life in exchange for a full explanation of his method. He rejected the offer and never did reveal his secret.

QUESTIONS

AUTHOR BIAS

1. The author of this selection believes that —

a. Bottineau had exceptional skills.
b. Bottineau's feats were not that unusual.
c. Bottineau was a fraud.

SELECTING CRITERIA

2. Which criterion does the selection rely mainly upon to evaluate Bottineau's feats?

a. Explanations given by Bottineau.
b. Number of successful predictions.
c. Use of method in gambling.

DETECTING ASSUMPTIONS

3. The author assumes that –

a. Bottineau was lucky.
b. Bottineau's method was easy to discover.
c. There was a secret to Bottineau's success.

8. Early Pistols

If everyone had pistols like the earliest ones, maybe fewer people would get shot. The earliest pistols were dangerous for the people who shot them as well as for the people at whom the pistols were aimed. The firing mechanism worked with a wheel wound up like a clock. When the trigger was pulled, the wheel ground against a stone and threw sparks. These sparks were supposed to ignite the gunpowder that fired the bullet.

This device was supposedly the invention of Camillo Ventelli of Italy in the 15th century. It wasn't too long before pistols began to compete with sabers and lances as the favorite weapons of soldiers on horseback. The horsemen found pistols easier to carry.

The pistol was invented for soldiers. But soon thieves, highwaymen, and assassins began to use pistols, too. A pistol could be hidden under a coat, then shot before anyone could stop the gunman.

Emperor Maximilian of the Holy Roman Empire outlawed the manufacture of pistols in 1517. A few years later, Parliament in England passed strict pistol-control laws to halt a troublesome crime wave.

The pistol got its name from Pistoria, Italy, the home town of the inventor. Pistols remained clumsy weapons, like other types of guns, until the end of the 1700's.

QUESTIONS

DETECTING ASSUMPTIONS

1. What appears to be a hidden assumption in the first sentence of the first paragraph?

a. A lot of people get shot by pistols.
b. Pistols can be safe weapons.
c. People should respect pistols.

CLASSIFICATION

2. Match.

______ Fired by means of wheel mechanism.	a. Pistol in 1550.
______ Uses shells.	b. Pistol in 1900.

RELEVANCE OF INFORMATION

3. The selection tells us that Maximilian outlawed the manufacture of pistols in 1517.
Which item of information from the selection is most relevant to Maximilian's decision?

a. The earliest pistols were dangerous to the people who fired them.
b. Soldiers on horseback began to use the new weapons.
c. Thieves, highwaymen, and assassins began to use pistols.

SELECTING CRITERIA

4. Which of the following characteristics of early pistols made them appealing to highwaymen? (Select one or more)

a. Their manufacture was illegal.
b. They could be hidden.
c. They were easy to carry.
d. They were invented by Camillo Ventelli.
e. They were dangerous to use.

CAUSE-EFFECT

5. Pulling the trigger caused the early pistol to fire. From information in the story, the pulling of the trigger was clearly —

a. A direct cause.
b. A necessary precondition.
c. An indirect cause.

9. The Beaver Is Still Busy

The beaver has been called "the animal that helped settle North America." In the 1600's, when white men began coming in large numbers to this country, the beaver's soft, shiny, warm fur was one of the things that attracted them. Indians trapped beavers and traded the beaver skins in exchange for European manufactured goods. Beaver fur was mainly used to make hats, and soon American beaver fur sat on the heads of millions of people in America and Europe. Europe went insane for beaver fur.

Soon white men began trapping beavers themselves. In Canada, French trappers known as *coureurs de bois*, or "woods runners," set up lonely trapping camps throughout the distant, wild country, first in the Great Lakes area and then further west all the way to the Pacific. From the mid-1600's through about 1850, their explorations helped open up much of Canada to settlement. In the United States, in the early 1800's, beaver trappers known as "mountain men" opened up the Rocky Mountains and the Far West in much the same way. So, in addition to making money for trappers, merchants, and hatters, beavers helped promote the exploration of large areas of land.

Beaver hunting became so widespread that by the late 1800's there were hardly any beavers left. Eventually, both the United States and Canada passed laws forbidding the taking of beavers, except for a short hunting season each year.

Gradually, the beavers returned. In a few places they became so plentiful that people began to think of them as pests. They built their dams on free-running streams and made ponds in inconvenient places. But today the beaver is being used to benefit mankind in a new way. In the late 1970's and early 1980's beavers were caught and transported to wilderness areas in the West. Wildlife specialists found areas where there were no longer fish and animals because the land had been changed too much. It had been transformed into pastures or cut up for mining. Its trees had been cut for lumber. But in one place after another, the imported beavers once again built dams to hold back water for ponds. Now with the help of the beavers the land is beginning to return to its natural state.

QUESTIONS

FIGURATIVE LANGUAGE

1. The last sentence in the first paragraph of this selection contains an example of –

a. Hyperbole
b. Personification
c. Simile

RELEVANCE OF INFORMATION

2. What information from the selection is most relevant to the statement that the beaver helped settle North America?

a. Information about the *coureurs de bois* and the "mountain men."
b. The laws forbidding the taking of beaver.
c. The description of the way beavers build dams.

EVALUATING CONCLUSIONS

3. In the last paragraph of the selection the author describes areas where the trees had been cut down, causing damage to the environment. The author states that with the help of beavers the land is beginning to return to its natural state.
What do you think of the implied logic here?

a. Good logic: When beavers build dams they help trees to grow.
b. Poor logic: Beavers cut down trees; they don't grow them.

CAUSE-EFFECT

4. "Beavers helped promote the exploration of large areas of land."
This sentence contains an example of—

a. A necessary precondition.
b. An indirect cause.
c. Multiple causes.

10. A Baffling Mystery

In 1960 astronomer Allan Sandage discovered something entirely new in the universe. Through very powerful telescopes it looked like a star. But Sandage's instruments told him that the object couldn't be a star. It was too far away. A star that far away would be invisible. Sandage named his discovery a *quasar*. Soon, like children who have been given a new toy, astronomers around the world turned to studying this strange new class of objects in the sky.

Quasars are objects that shine with a brilliance 1,000 times greater than our entire Milky Way galaxy, but are only the size of a large star. Their fierce glow is so irregular that astronomers have not been able to determine exactly how far away they are or what provides their light.

Scientists have learned that light sent from any object traveling away from us becomes less visible and more red in color. This "shift to red" is used as a method of measuring motion in space: The more distant an object is, the faster it is traveling away from us. Quasars possess the greatest red shift of any object in the heavens. This fact suggests that quasars are in the most remote and ancient parts of the universe. If this is so, they could tell us secrets about the universe's beginnings.

There is a problem with this idea. If quasars are so far away, how can they be so bright? Some astronomers think this is impossible, so the quasars must really be near our own galaxy. In that case the red shifts are leading us astray.

What the astronomers are looking for is some object whose brightness can be accurately measured as it moves away. Some scientists may be on the right track because they are refiguring the distance of quasars. In a few years, we may know the "secret" of these strange objects in the sky.

QUESTIONS

FIGURATIVE LANGUAGE

1. The last sentence in the first paragraph contains an example of —

a. Hyperbole.
b. Personification.
c. Simile.

AUTHOR BIAS

2. What is the bias of the author of this selection?

a. Favors the theory that quasars are in the most distant parts of the universe.
b. Favors the theory that quasars are near our own galaxy.
c. Is neutral.

SELECTING CRITERIA

3. Match.

____ Suggests quasars are near our galaxy.	a. Brightness
____ Suggests quasars are very distant.	b. Red shift

CLASSIFICATION

4. The selection states that quasars are classed differently from stars because they shine with a brilliance 1,000 times greater than our Milky Way.

This is an example of classification on the basis of —

a. Physical characteristics
b. Uses/Functions
c. Time/Place

5. Paragraph 4 contains the statement that "quasars must be near our own galaxy."

What is the key word that makes this generalization highly limiting?

____

Reading & Critical Thinking, Book 2

Teacher's Guide • Answer Key

Description

Educational Design's **Reading and Critical Thinking 2** is a skillbook that teaches 10 more advanced critical thinking skills associated with reading. (Less advanced skills, or skills taught at a less advanced level, are covered in a companion skillbook, *Reading and Critical Thinking 1*.) Each of these 10 skills is taught in a separate chapter. The chapters are organized into three main sections as follows:

A. Literal Reading Skills
   1. Cause—Effect Relationships

B. Inferential Thinking Skills
   2. Detecting Assumptions and Evaluating Conclusions
   3. Classifying Ideas, Objects, People, and Events
   4. Detecting Confusing Problems with Words
   5. Selecting Criteria for Use in Making Judgments
   6. Figurative Language

C. Evaluative Thinking Skills
   7. Problems with Generalizations
   8. Judging the Relevance of Information
   9. Analyzing Persuasive Techniques
   10. Author Bias

Each chapter introduces a skill in the same way. First there is specific instruction on the skill, followed by a series of exercise questions that are typically based on brief descriptive paragraphs of reading matter. (Answers to these exercises appear in the book boxed and upside down.) This instructional material is in turn followed in the chapter by three or more 300- to 500-word selections, each with its own set of exercise questions that develop students' understanding of the skill being taught. (Answers to these questions appear at the end of the present Teacher's Guide.)

Very few books for reading instruction actually teach the way the chapters in this book do. Most reading books typically contain reading selections followed by comprehension questions. **Reading and Critical Thinking**, on the other hand, actually leads students step by step to an understanding of each of the skills presented. The authors feel that this didactic approach toward reading instruction will become more and more important in the years ahead.

Following the 10 instructional chapters is **Section D: Putting It All Together**, which contains 10 additional reading selections, each followed by exercises which test on a combination of the skills taught in this book.

The entire book thus contains 45 specially prepared full reading selections (three or more for each of the 10 skills taught plus an additional 10 selections that test on a combination of skills). Reading levels are 6 to 8, while content is at a mature level. The book will appeal to a broad audience of secondary and adult students, including both average students and those in need of remediation.

Purpose

There is a growing interest among educators in the relationship between thought and reading. It is more and more recognized that good readers are active readers.

They think as they read. They maintain a dialogue with what they read, constantly bringing to bear their own experiences, opinions and background and trying to place written material in perspective.

Unfortunately, many students who have mastered decoding and deciphering skills have trouble going much beyond this, even in comprehending much more than a few sentences at a time. In plain language, they do not think about what they are reading as they read it. Or they soak up information uncritically, without considering such matters as whether a piece of writing is logical and consistent, or whether its generalizations are fair and accurate, or whether the author's bias is shaping what the piece of writing says. Or, if they do exercise these critical reading skills, they do not exercise them in a controlled or systematic way.

The purpose of this book is to introduce your students to a variety of reading/thinking skills and to provide an organizational framework for their development. But the mastery of good reading/thinking skills is the result of an ongoing process. Students who have worked through this book will need continuing instruction in the skills taught: through classroom instruction; through group discussion of material which has been read; and in the application of the same skills to the teaching of writing.

Students who develop good reading/thinking skills become better readers. These skills are really central to reading comprehension. And as a corollary, they are of tremendous importance in reading tests. They lead to better comprehension of reading material no matter what the context. And they are among the skills that are required for good writing.

About the Authors

Donald Barnes, Ed. D., is Professor of Education, Teachers College, Ball State University, and a specialist in reading pedagogy. Dr. Barnes also has extensive experience in elementary and secondary teaching at grade levels 3 through 11, both in the U.S. and abroad.

His collaborator, Arlene Burgdorf, Ed.D., has a broad background as teacher, supervisor, and principal in the Hammond, Ind., public schools.

Dr. Barnes and Dr. Burgdorf have worked together on numerous projects and are the authors of more than 100 publications in the field of reading instruction.

Answer Key

1. Cause–Effect Relationships

RACING OVER THE ICE (p. 7)
1. being in good physical condition, being able to sleep in the cold, getting financial support, getting ships and supplies, etc.
2. Peary's reaching the North Pole led to Amundsen's changing his destination from the North to the South Pole.
3. storms, cold, semi-darkness, dangerous terrain, hunger (Scott only).

MICROWAVE MANIA (p. 8)
1. no valid cause
2. only one of many causes
3. indirect cause
4. no valid cause
5. no valid cause
6. necessary precondition

(other answers to 2, 3, and 6 may be reasonable)

A LIGHTNING CURE (p. 9)
1. b, c (if the tree attracted the lightning bolt), d, f
2. a, b, c

STOPPED BY A METEORITE (p. 10)
1. c, b, a
2. b
3. b
4. a, b, c, g

2. Detecting Assumptions and Evaluating Conclusions

THE MYSTERY OF THE BERMUDA TRIANGLE (p. 15)
1. a
2. destruction by enemies, strange forces at work, defective ships and planes, multiple causes, including the above, etc.
3. Your opinion—no correct answer. However, there is no known flying monster that can destroy planes, and it is difficult to imagine where one would hide, live, and breed, as well as what it would eat.
4. Your opinion—no correct answer. However, if you believe the UFO explanation, you should be prepared to explain why they destroy so many planes over the Bermuda Triangle and nowhere else.

HIGH-TECH CERAMICS (p. 16)
1. a
2. a
3. b
4. b
5. a
6. c
7. yes

A TECHNICAL TRIUMPH (p. 17)
1. a
2. a
3. yes

THE GREAT STORM OF 1913 (p. 18)
1. c
2. The story mentions icy waves and men freezing to death.
3. c
4. Your opinion—no correct answer. An even greater storm might possibly happen, and cause equally great damage. But the author states only that a storm causing such damage is unlikely, not impossible.

3. Classifying Ideas, Objects, People, and Events

SHOES THROUGH THE AGES (p. 25)
1. c, d, e, a, b
2. b
3. c
4. a
5. I. orthopedic, boots, slippers; II. laced, pointed-toe, oxford; III. narrow widths; IV. expensive, bargain

EDIBLE EXPLOSIONS (p. 26)
1. b
2. popcorn
3. b
4. b

INTGLSAT (p. 28)
1. c
2. a
3. b
4. a = II, b = IV, c = I
5. a, b, e (and d, if you consider something like "Intelsat III" to be a name.)
6. A. Retired in 1969, "Early Bird"; B. Deploy date 1966–1967, 240 two-way voice transmissions; C. Deploy date 1968–1970, 8 satellites; D. 9,000 phone circuits, 8 satellites, 12 color television broadcasts

4. Detecting Confusing Problems with Words

TALE OF UNBELIEVABLE DISASTERS (p. 35)
1. b
2. a
3. b
4. b
5. c

HOLDING THINGS TOGETHER (p. 36)
1. b, c, f
2. c
3. c
4. c
5. b
6. a
7. b
8. b
9. a

EYEGLASSES (p. 38)
1. b
2. a
3. a
4. b
5. a
6. a
7. a
8. b

5. Selecting Criteria for Use in Making Judgments

POON LIM'S RECORD (p. 41)
1. a, b, d, e (these are 4 possibilities; you only need 3)
2. c

A DOG'S LIFE (p. 42)
1. c, d, a, b, b, d

THE LONGEST RACE IN HISTORY (p. 43)
1. time he took, his average speed, how much he beat the runner-up by
2. payment of entry fee, length of race, location of terminus, specific route followed, how prize money was to be divided, specified distances that had to be run each day, method of determining winners. (You only need 3)

6. Figurative Language

SHE FELL SIX MILES (p. 46)
1. a
2. a
3. a
4. S, P, S, S, P

GLORY, DEFEAT, GLORY AGAIN (p. 47)
1. a
2. c
3. b
4. b

WAGING WAR ON SOUTHERN MOSQUITOES (p. 48)
1a. S (H might also be correct)
b. H
c. P
d. P
e. H
f. H
g. P

7. Problems with Generalizations

SKIING OVER BACTERIA (p. 52)
1a. All
b. never
c. always
d. Nobody
e. Every
f. Only
g. always
h. No . . . ever
i. never
j. only

A CONTINUING LOVE AFFAIR (p. 53)
1. b
2. b
3. b
4. a
5. b
6. a
7. b
8. b

"BAT" MASTERSON (p. 54)
1. c, d, b, a

8. Judging the Relevance of Information

A LONELY TRIP TO THE POLE (p. 57)
1. b
2. a

LEARNING TO SURVIVE AT SEA (p. 57)
1. c
2. b

USING LIGHT FOR CONVERSATIONS (p. 58)
1. b
2. b

ELECTRIC CARS AGAIN (p. 59)
1. c
2. b
3. c

KIRLIAN PHOTOGRAPHY (p. 60)
1. b, d, a, c
2. c
3. b

ANIMAL OR PLANT (p. 61)
1. a
2. a
3. a

9. Analyzing Persuasive Techniques

A LETTER FROM *CITIZENS TO HELP THE POOR* (p. 65)
1. a
2. c
3. c (b is also possible, but see Question 4)
4. b

IF I'M ELECTED . . . (p. 66)
1a. Top Quality
b. Showing You Care
c. Avoiding Failure
2. c
3. c
4. a

A WORD FROM OUR SPONSOR (p. 68)
1. c
2. b
3. b
4. c, a, b
5. c

10. Author Bias

WOLVES (p. 71)
1. loyalty, intelligence, friendliness
2. The ruination of Tim Perry's ranch by wolves.
3. "the Consitutional right" to protect one's property (a "right" that is not actually in the Constitution).

AN UNREALIZED DREAM (p. 72)
1. a
2. a
3a. superstition, guesswork, etc.
b. silly people, ignorant fakers, deluded fools, ineffective dabblers, etc.
4. experiments
5. usual energy

A LIMITED MIRACLE (p. 74)
1. c
2. a
3. a
4. a
5. c
6. P, N
7. N, P
8. N, P

D. Putting It All Together

UNDERWATER DISCOVERIES (p. 77)

1. a
2. The firmness of the Japanese army; the Japanese attack on and the burning of the Mongol ships; the sinking of the Mongol ships by the typhoon
3. All

TREMBLING HANDS THAT SEE (p. 79)

1. a

2a. appeal to scientific authority (or equivalent answer).

b. the locating of Mrs. Kulckhohn's lost bag by a hand trembler.

3. a
4. b
5. b

UNSUNG HEROES (p. 81)

1. b
2. a
3. 102-degree temperature, 100-percent humidity.
4. b

A UNIQUE MUSCLE (p. 83)

1. c, a, b
2. c, c, a
3. organ, buds, fork
4. a

A TOOTHLESS SPINEBALL (p. 85)

1. c
2. a
3. b
4. b
5. a
6. b

INEXPENSIVE PROPERTY (p. 87)

1. a, c, b
2. a
3. c
4. a

NAUSCOPIE (p. 89)

1. a
2. b
3. c

EARLY PISTOLS (p. 91)

1. a
2. a, b
3. c
4. b, c
5. c

THE BEAVER IS STIL[illegible] (p. 93)

1. a (b is also possible [illegible]nly people go insane)
2. a
3. a
4. c

A BAFFLING MYSTERY

1. c
2. c
3. a, b
4. a
5. must